101 VIDEO GAMES

TO PLAY BEFORE YOU GROW UP

THE UNOFFICIAL MUST-PLAY
VIDEO GAME LIST FOR KIDS

CONSOLE QUICK GUIDE

DC—SEGA Dreamcast
GB—Game Boy
GBA—Game Boy Advance
GC—GameCube
iOS—Apple devices
NES—Nintendo Entertainment System
N64—Nintendo 64
PC—Microsoft personal computer
PS—PlayStation (Original, 2, 3, 4, Portable, Vita)
SNES—Super Nintendo Entertainment System
X360—Xbox 360
XOne—Xbox One
(All other system names are unabbreviated.)

Brimming with creative inspiration, how-to projects, and useful information to enrich your everyday life, Quarto Knows is a favorite destination for those pursuing their interests and passions. Visit our site and dig deeper with our books into your area of interest: Quarto Creates, Quarto Cooks, Quarto Homes, Quarto Lives, Quarto Drives, Quarto Explores, Quarto Gifts, or Quarto Kids.

© 2017 Quarto Publishing Group USA Inc.
Illustrations © Spencer Wilson

First Published in 2017 by Walter Foster Jr., an imprint of The Quarto Group.
6 Orchard Road, Suite 100, Lake Forest, CA 92630, USA.
T (949) 380-7510 **F** (949) 380-7575 **www.QuartoKnows.com**

Walter Foster Jr. titles are also available at discount for retail, wholesale, promotional, and bulk purchase. For details, contact the Special Sales Manager by email at specialsales@quarto.com or by mail at The Quarto Group, Attn: Special Sales Manager, 401 Second Avenue North, Suite 310, Minneapolis, MN 55401 USA.

This book is an independent, unauthorized, and unofficial guide and is not endorsed or sponsored by Nintendo Co., Ltd.; Activision Publishing, Inc.; Microsoft Corp.; BANDAI NAMCO Entertainment America Inc.; Insomniac Games, Inc.; Sony Interactive Entertainment America, LLC; Media Molecule; Capcom, Ltd.; Ubisoft Entertainment; SEGA; MOJANG; WayForward; Technologies Inc.; Double Fine Productions, Inc.; Yacht Club Games, LLC; Studio Pixel; Konami Gaming, Inc.; DrinkBox Studios; TT Games; LucasArts Entertainment Company, LLC; Rollingmedia; Electronic Arts Inc.; Take-Two Interactive Software, Inc.; Psyonix, Inc.; Camelot Games; SQUARE ENIX Ltd.; Undertale (Toby Fox); Level-5 Inc.; Natsume Inc.; Blizzard Entertainment, Inc.; Tetris Holding; Sirvo Studios, LLC; Valve Corp.; Jupiter Corp.; Rovio Entertainment Ltd.; Harmonix Music Systems, Inc.; NanaOn-Sha Co., Ltd.; Gaijin Entertainment; or any other person or entity owning or controlling rights in their name, trademark, or copyrights.

Trademarks, trade names, and characters depicted and referred to herein are the property of their respective owners and are used solely to identify the particular video game or games with which each such trademark, trade name or character is associated.

ISBN: 978-1-60058-785-6

Written by Ben Bertoli

Printed in China
10 9 8 7 6 5 4 3 2 1

MIX
Paper from responsible sources
FSC® C101537
www.fsc.org

101 VIDEO GAMES

TO PLAY BEFORE YOU GROW UP

The ratings listed in this book reflect the complete range of ratings given by the Entertainment Software Rating Board (ESRB) for individual games in the series.

A NOTE FROM THE AUTHOR

I've played every game in this book. (It's an awesome job, and someone's got to do it!) Of course, even with all the hours I've spent playing these games and my most earnest efforts to double check every detail, games are always changing, and I may have made a few errors. If they exist, I hope they are few and far between. The best way to know if a game is right for you is to talk with your parents and try playing it yourself. Use the prompts to rate all 101 games on my list, and you'll be a winner in my book!

WRITTEN BY BEN BERTOLI
ILLUSTRATED BY SPENCER WILSON

TABLE OF CONTENTS

GENRES

Action—Prepare for explosive encounters and lots of excitement

Adventure—Embark on epic journeys and memorable battles

Arcade—Go old school with retro graphics and simple gameplay

Fighting—Throw down with crazy characters and attacks

Party—Grab your friends and let the good times roll

Platformer—Hop and bop through adventures with colorful heroes

Puzzle—Think fast and test your reflexes

Rhythm—Get your groove on with music-based games

Role Playing—Take on a new life and brave legendary quests

Sports—Compete in digital versions of real and made-up sports

Strategy—Plan every move carefully to conquer the game

1

SUPER MARIO BROS.

PLAY IT ON:
Switch, Wii U,
3DS, and more

GENRE:
Platformer

RATING:
E

**FIRST
SEEN:**
1985

MADE BY:
Nintendo

One of the most influential and well-known gaming series of all time, Super Mario Bros. has been delighting and challenging the world for over 30 years. The series was created by Shigeru Miyamoto, who has worked on every single Mario adventure since the pudgy plumbers' original 8-bit outing in the mid '80s.

The first Super Mario Bros. game for NES had Mario moving from left to right toward a flagpole at the end of each level. To reach his goal, Mario had to make daring jumps and take down enemies, collecting coins and power-ups along the way. All 2D Super Mario Bros. titles followed these basic guidelines, adding new power-ups and baddies, as well as showcasing outrageous new levels. In 1996, Mario made the jump to 3D with the release of *Super Mario 64*. Since then, he has starred in both 2D and 3D platformers for almost every Nintendo system created.

Many of the power-ups and other items Mario collects in the series are iconic in the gaming community, including the super mushroom, the super star, the fire flower, and more. Mario often takes on different forms when he powers up, and has been known to don different colored overalls, as well as animal-related suits, including bees, frogs, cats, and most famously, the Japanese raccoon dogs known as tanuki.

Mario and his younger brother Luigi live in the Mushroom Kingdom, a fantastical world ruled by Mario's damsel in distress, Princess Peach. The evil Bowser, known as King Koopa in Japan, is always trying to get his hands on the princess and steal her away from Mario. Over the years, Mario has fought Bowser on tropical islands, in dark dungeons, and even in space!

DID YOU KNOW?

According to the instructions for the first *Super Mario Bros.*, all the brick blocks in the game are actually Mushroom Kingdom citizens who've been cursed by Bowser—meaning Mario was accidentally smashing all the people he was trying to save. Oh no!

WHAT TO PLAY NEXT:
The Kirby series
The Rayman series
The Mega Man series

TOP SERIES PICKS:
Super Mario Bros. 3 (NES, 1988)
Super Mario 64 (N64, 1996)
Super Mario Galaxy (Wii, 2007)

YOU'LL LIKE THESE GAMES IF...
You have a spring in your step!

Played it! ☐   My Rating: ☆☆☆☆☆

My Favorite Moment: _____

Notes: _____

_____

2

YOSHI

PLAY IT ON:
Wii U, 3DS,
SNES, and more

GENRE:
Platformer

RATING:
E

**FIRST
SEEN:**
1995

MADE BY:
Nintendo

Yoshi first appeared on the scene when he was introduced as Mario's dinosaur friend in *Super Mario World* for Super Nintendo. Gamers were so impressed with his ability to gobble up Mario's foes that Nintendo decided Yoshi should star in the next Mario title. While the game was in the works, two Yoshi puzzle games were quickly produced for the original NES and Game Boy.

In 1995, *Super Mario World 2: Yoshi's Island* was introduced with a unique cartoonish look and a charming soundtrack. With a variety of new moves, including the ability to use his long tongue to slurp up baddies and turn them into eggs, Yoshi is in charge of a helpless baby Mario. As players make their way through the island's many levels, they use Yoshi's egg-tossing ability to hit switches, coins, enemies, and more—a classic Yoshi move throughout the series.

The most recent title, *Yoshi's Woolly World* for the Wii U and 3DS, takes place in a setting created entirely of craft materials. Bosses unravel, levels come apart at the seams, and colorful balls of yarn can be used to wrap up any trouble that crosses Yoshi's adorable path.

DID YOU KNOW?

According to *Super Mario World* director Takashi Tezuka, Yoshi was originally going to be a koopa (one of the turtle enemies in the Mario games). That's why his red saddle resembles a shell.

Played it! ☐   My Rating: ☆☆☆☆☆

My Favorite Moment: _____

Notes: _____

_____

DONKEY KONG COUNTRY

3

Starring one of gaming's most notorious arcade villains, Donkey Kong Country games task players with collecting bananas, tossing barrels, and literally rolling over the competition in search of DK's stolen banana hoard. To win, players must track down and defeat the fiendish King K. Rool.

The first three games in the series use pre-rendered graphics, a type of 3D visual effect that made the games stand out from competitors. They also feature some of the best soundtracks in gaming history! Although each game includes the name Donkey Kong in the title, the big ape himself is only playable in the first adventure. Later games introduce new Kongs, including Diddy Kong, Dixie Kong, and Kiddy Kong. Other Kong family members, such as Cranky Kong and Funky Kong, show up to help players save their progress and move from world to world.

In 2010 Nintendo launched *Donkey Kong Country Returns* on Wii. Donkey and Diddy Kong, the original kings of swing, returned as the heroes in this new adventure. The game was a big hit with fans and was eventually ported to the 3DS for handheld play. A sequel to *Returns* came to the Wii U in 2014 and was dubbed *Donkey Kong Country: Tropical Freeze*. Sounds refreshing, doesn't it?

PLAY IT ON:
Wii U, 3DS, SNES, and more

GENRE:
Platformer

RATING:
E

FIRST SEEN:
1994

MADE BY:
Nintendo

DID YOU KNOW?

When players visit Wrinkly Kong to save their progress in *Donkey Kong Country 3*, they can see her playing *Super Mario 64* on her very own Nintendo 64 system!

Played it! ☐   My Rating: ☆☆☆☆☆
My Favorite Moment: _____
Notes: _____
_____

4

KIRBY

PLAY IT ON:
Wii U, 3DS, DS,
and more

GENRE:
Platformer

RATING:
E

**FIRST
SEEN:**
1992

MADE BY:
Nintendo

Kirby is best known for being a floating pink puffball that steals the powers of his opponents. After the success of *Kirby's Dream Land*, his first game for Game Boy, Nintendo released *Kirby's Adventure* for the NES in 1993. Despite being released on NES two years after the launch of the Super NES, the game sold very well, and we've been playing Kirby titles on Nintendo handhelds and consoles ever since.

Starting with *Kirby's Adventure*, almost all Kirby titles have featured his signature power to gobble up baddies and use their abilities. Kirby may look cute and cuddly, but when he is supercharged with electricity or ice, he can hurt anyone in his way. All Kirby adventures are side-scrolling platformers with a focus on saving Dream Land or Kirby's home planet, Pop Star, from devious villains. Often Kirby's adversaries are Dream Land regulars Meta Knight and King Dedede, though many times they team up with the pink puff to help save the day.

Not every game gives Kirby his signature power. In *Kirby Canvas Curse* for the DS and *Kirby and the Rainbow Curse* for the Wii U, the Dream Land hero is transformed into a ball and players have to draw magic paths for him to roll on. In the most recent Kirby game, *Kirby: Planet Robobot* for the 3DS, Kirby dons a mech suit that can enhance his stolen powers to the max—nothing says, "Take me seriously!" like piloting a giant robot with a flamethrower.

DID YOU KNOW?

Although Kirby is known for his cuteness, box art for games outside of Japan consistently portray him as angry and serious. Series director Shinya Kumazaki says this is because global audiences like their characters "tough."

WHAT TO PLAY NEXT:
The Yoshi series
The LittleBigPlanet series
The Legendary Starfy

TOP SERIES PICKS:
Kirby's Dream Land 2 (GB, 1999)
Kirby Super Star Ultra (DS, 2008)
Kirby: Planet Robobot (3DS, 2016)

YOU'LL LIKE THESE GAMES IF...
You love to gobble up tasty treats.

Played it! ☐   My Rating: ☆☆☆☆☆

My Favorite Moment: _____

Notes: _____

_____

5

CRASH BANDICOOT

PLAY IT ON:
PS4, PS2, PS, and more

GENRE:
Platformer

RATING:
E

FIRST SEEN:
1996

MADE BY:
Naughty Dog

With Mario representing Nintendo and Sonic starring at SEGA, the folks at Sony were on the lookout for their own mascot. They found one in *Crash Bandicoot*, a platforming title developed by Naughty Dog. The game focuses on a wacky marsupial and his quest to stop the mad scientist who created him. Crash is known for his quick spins, high bounces, and belly flops. He bashes crates and collects delicious Wumpa fruit as he escapes the grasp of the evil Dr. Neo Cortex. Unlike many 3D platformers of the '90s, the Crash games feature liner levels, meaning there isn't a big world to roam around in, there's only a general path from start to finish that players follow to reach their goal.

Family and friends help Crash on his adventures throughout the Wumpa Islands. His most helpful companion is Aku Aku, a witch doctor spirit who takes the form of a wooden mask with feathers. Collecting Aku Aku's many masks can momentarily shield Crash from enemies and even make him invincible. Crash's sister Coco is introduced in his second game. She helps her brother by completing levels that involve strange forms of transportation, such as jet skis and her pet tiger Pura.

The Crash series has been through many developers and publishers since the original three games. In fact, no one had seen Crash in a console adventure for nearly ten years when it was announced he would be returning, both in his own HD collection for PS4 in 2017 and as a special character for the Skylanders series in 2016. Bandi*woot*!

DID YOU KNOW?
According to developer Dave Baggett, the fictional Wumpa fruit that Crash collects taste like apples.

WHAT TO PLAY NEXT:
The Spyro series
The Jak and Daxter series
The Banjo-Kazooie series

TOP SERIES PICKS:
Crash Bandicoot (PS, 1996)
Crash Bandicoot 3: Warped
(PS, 1998)
Crash Bandicoot N. Sane Trilogy
(PS4, 2017)

YOU'LL LIKE THESE GAMES IF...
You love twisted Australian animals.

Played it! ☐   My Rating: ☆☆☆☆☆☆

My Favorite Moment: _____

Notes: _____

_____

6

SPYRO

PLAY IT ON:
PS3, PS2, PS,
and more

GENRE:
Platformer

RATING:
E–E10+

**FIRST
SEEN:**
1998

MADE BY:
Insomniac
Games

While Crash Bandicoot was seen as PlayStation's temporary mascot, the bigwigs at Sony still felt like there weren't enough family-friendly titles for their system. Insomniac Games was tasked with creating a new platforming title that anyone could enjoy. They eventually chose a dragon as their hero, and the rest is gaming history.

The first Spyro game is set in the Dragon Kingdom, a world sectioned into five different realms. After being insulted by a resident of the Dragon Kingdom on TV, Gnasty Gnorc decides to teach the big lizards a lesson by trapping them in crystal statues. Only Spyro manages to escape the curse and must step up to save the day. By collecting gems and dragon eggs, Spyro can open new realms and discover secrets hidden throughout the Dragon Kingdom.

Fans know Spyro may be a dragon, but he's lacking a bit in the fire and flying departments. He does manage to spew small bursts of flames at enemies and use his small wings to glide from platform to platform. Some stages even let Spyro fly for long periods of time so he can collect relics and reach new heights!

DID YOU KNOW?

Designers first made Spyro green, but they changed his scales to an eye-popping purple when he kept blending into grassy backgrounds.

Played it! ☐   My Rating: ☆☆☆☆☆
My Favorite Moment: _____
Notes: _____
_____

BANJO-KAZOOIE

The development team at Rare was riding high with best-selling series Donkey Kong Country. Their next title was released on Nintendo 64 and featured the hero Banjo and a sassy red bird known as Kazooie. The story of the original game focuses on Banjo and Kazooie's quest to save Banjo's sister Tooty from the clutches of the repulsive witch Gruntilda. The two heroes are assisted by an educated mole named Bottles and a selfish shaman named Mumbo. To unlock new areas, players must find golden puzzle pieces known as Jiggies and shiny musical notes that are scattered across the game's many worlds.

After the success of *Banjo-Tooie* (also for the Nintendo 64), there were rumors that a third title named *Banjo Threeie* was in the works. Unfortunately, Microsoft bought Rare, and they began working on new projects for the Xbox home console. Eventually they announced a game for the Xbox 360: *Banjo-Kazooie: Nuts & Bolts*, which focuses more on building vehicles than the outstanding platforming the series was once known for. But the spirit of *Banjo-Kazooie* still lives! In 2017, a group of former Rare developers released *Yooka-Laylee*, which has struck a chord with fans of the original series.

DID YOU KNOW?

Banjo first showed up as a playable driver in the game *Diddy Kong Racing*, another Nintendo 64 title from Rare.

PLAY IT ON:
XOne, X360, N64, and more

GENRE:
Platformer

RATING:
E–E10+

FIRST SEEN:
1998

MADE BY:
Rare

Played it! ☐   My Rating: ☆☆☆☆☆
My Favorite Moment: _____
Notes: _____
_____

8

KLONOA

PLAY IT ON:
Wii, PS3, PSVita, and more

GENRE:
Platformer

RATING:
E–E10+

FIRST SEEN:
1997

MADE BY:
Namco

What do you call a game that has 3D graphics but only lets characters move in two directions? The answer is 2.5D, of course! Klonoa was one of the first console games to use this trick. While all the characters and backgrounds are made of 3D models, the game only allows players to move side to side and up and down on a scrolling path. Many game series—including Super Mario Bros., Donkey Kong Country, and LittleBigPlanet—use this same trick to give players stunning visuals while literally keeping them on track.

As a Dream Traveler, it's Klonoa's duty to protect different dream worlds and bring them peace. Using his special ring, known as the Wind Bullet, he grabs enemies and blows away any foes that stand in his path. In the first two games, he must save the mythical lands of Phantomile and Lunatea from evildoers who want to harness the power of dreams for themselves.

Though it started as a PlayStation exclusive, there have been a handful of games with Klonoa for the Game Boy Advance and a Japanese handheld known as the WonderSwann. Who knows, maybe Klonoa will show up in YOUR dreams!

DID YOU KNOW?

Pac-Man, the famous arcade ghost muncher, can be seen on Klonoa's hat. It's a clever nod to the fact that both Klonoa and Pac-Man titles are made by Namco.

Played it! ☐   My Rating: ☆☆☆☆☆

My Favorite Moment: _____

Notes: _____

_____

KID ICARUS

If you're up for a challenge, then Kid Icarus is for you; only the best players can master this classic Nintendo series. The original games borrow from both platformer and adventure series, while the most recent title includes some stellar flying stages.

The story of *Kid Icarus* is loosely based on Greek mythology. It follows Pit, a young angel dedicated to rescuing Palutena the Goddess of Light from the clutches of the demented Medusa. Pit must escape the Underworld and recover three sacred treasures using limited flight and his trusty bow. Along the way, he faces bizarre creatures, including food-based wizards who try to turn Pit into an eggplant or tempura (a breaded type of Japanese shrimp).

Though Pit hadn't been a playable character since 1991's *Kid Icarus: Of Myths and Monsters* for Game Boy, he still made the cut to be on the *Super Smash Bros. Brawl* roster in 2008. With this newfound stardom, the cult status behind the Kid Icarus games grew, and Nintendo began work on a new Kid Icarus title for their upcoming 3DS. After over 20 years of waiting, fans got *Kid Icarus: Uprising*, a fully 3D, on-the-rails, shooter-adventure game with intensity levels like "White Hot" and "Extra Spicy!"

DID YOU KNOW?

Despite many video games being exclusive to Japan, *Kid Icarus: Of Myths and Monsters* was never released there. It was 21 years later on the 3DS virtual console that the game was finally released to Japanese players.

PLAY IT ON:
Wii U, 3DS, GB, and more

GENRE:
Platformer

RATING:
E–E10+

FIRST SEEN:
1986

MADE BY:
Nintendo

Played it! ☐   My Rating: ☆☆☆☆☆

My Favorite Moment: _____

Notes: _____

_____

10

RATCHET AND CLANK

PLAY IT ON:
PS4, PS3, PS2,
and more

GENRE:
Platformer

RATING:
E10+–T

**FIRST
SEEN:**
2002

MADE BY:
Insomniac
Games

After the success of their Spyro series on the original PlayStation, Insomniac Games set out to create their first big hit for PlayStation 2. Ratchet and Clank premiered on Sony's new system in 2002 to rave reviews from fans and critics alike. The game went on to inspire more than ten sequels and a full-length feature film.

The series begins on the far-off planet of Veldin, where players are introduced to a crafty interstellar mechanic known as Ratchet. Ratchet, a short cat-like alien called a Lombax, is thought to be the last of his kind. It isn't long until Ratchet meets up with an escaped robot who goes by the charming name of XJ-0461. Ratchet dubs this helpful robot *Clank*, and the two team up to save the universe. While Ratchet can be brash and unpredictable, Clank is always calm and intellectual. Their teamwork and comedic dialogue are some of the best in gaming. They often find themselves in the company of the unbearable Captain Qwark, a celebrated space hero who is more concerned about publicity than actual heroism.

An arsenal of ridiculous weaponry makes the Ratchet and Clank series stand out from other platformers. Fan favorites include the Groovibomb Glove (a booty-shaking distraction that leaves enemies defenseless), the Morph-O-Ray (which turns baddies into barnyard animals), and Mr. Zurkon (a deadly robot ally who taunts opponents as he blasts them to bits). Every new Ratchet and Clank title is chock-full of crazy new gadgets and funky firepower. The series saw a reboot in 2016, so hopefully a new adventure is in the works for everyone's favorite interstellar duo.

WHAT TO PLAY NEXT:
The Jak and Daxter series
The Sly Cooper series
Psychonauts

TOP SERIES PICKS:
Ratchet and Clank: Up Your Arsenal (PS2, 2004)
Ratchet and Clank Future: Tools of Destruction (PS3, 2007)
Ratchet and Clank (PS4, 2016)

DID YOU KNOW?
Before he was a cat-like Lombax, Ratchet was designed as a goggle-wearing reptile with extendable arms and a thick tail.

YOU'LL LIKE THESE GAMES IF...
You think wacky weapons are the best.

Played it! ☐   My Rating: ☆☆☆☆☆

My Favorite Moment: _____

Notes: _____

_____

11

SLY COOPER

PLAY IT ON:
PSVita, PS3,
and PS2

GENRE:
Platformer

RATING:
E–E10+

**FIRST
SEEN:**
2002

MADE BY:
Sucker Punch

If you're going to make a game about the ultimate thief, why not make the star a critter that's known for stealing? In the first title, players learn that Sly comes from a long line of sticky-fingered raccoons that follow the teachings of a legendary book known as *The Thievius Raccoonus*. When the book is stolen from his family, and his father is killed in the resulting struggle, Sly vows to avenge his father and return the book to its home. Years later, Sly teams up with his friends to pull off his master caper. Bentley, a know-it-all turtle with a tendency to worry, is the brains of the operation. Murray, an ever-hungry hippo with some serious strength, provides the muscle and handles the driving. The Cooper Gang works together to steal back Sly's family heirloom from the grubby mitts of The Fiendish Five.

Sly games are all about stealth. Like any good thief, he knows when to hide in the shadows and when to strike. Players guide the masked raccoon as he infiltrates various locations with his trusty hooked cane. Each sequel to the original title finds Sly and the gang with a new master plan and relics to be snatched.

DID YOU KNOW?

Sly's devilishly handsome voice wasn't always so smooth. The thieving raccoon originally talked with a stereotypical Brooklyn accent.

Played it! ☐   My Rating: ☆☆☆☆☆

My Favorite Moment: _____

Notes: _____

_____

JAK AND DAXTER

Before the likes of Ratchet and Sly Cooper appeared, Jak and Daxter were the kings of otherworldly adventures. The first Jak and Daxter title launched just over a year after Sony's PS2 and was quickly a certified hit.

In the flagship game, players are first introduced to Jak and Daxter as they explore the mysterious and forbidden Misty Island. After a run-in with a monster known as a lurker, Daxter accidentally falls into a pit of noxious energy called Dark Eco. When Daxter emerges, his human body has been transformed into an ottsel (a combination of otter and weasel). To reverse the curse and stop the other lurkers from releasing more Dark Eco upon the world, Jak and Daxter set off to find the Dark Sage.

Though most combat is reliant on close-up melee attacks, Jak is eventually suited up with a Morph Gun that can change based on the different colors of Eco. The series also focuses on driving crazy vehicles, such as flying cars and dune-buggy-like rovers. We haven't seen Jak and Daxter since their collection came to PS3, so here's hoping they'll team up again in the near future. Just don't visit your local zoo hoping to see an ottsel.

PLAY IT ON:
PSVita, PS3, PS2, and more

GENRE:
Platformer

RATING:
E–T

FIRST SEEN:
2001

DID YOU KNOW?

There are hidden pictures of Ratchet and Clank in many of the Jak and Daxter games. Ratchet is even a secret playable driver in the racing game *Jak X*.

MADE BY:
Naughty Dog

Played it! ☐   My Rating: ☆☆☆☆☆

My Favorite Moment: _____

Notes: _____

_____

13 LITTLEBIGPLANET

PLAY IT ON:
PS4, PSVita, PS3,
and more

GENRE:
Platformer

RATING:
E

**FIRST
SEEN:**
2008

MADE BY:
Media Molecule

There are plenty of games that let players pick their own silly details, but LittleBigPlanet introduced a new level of customization and intricate crafting tools that the world had never seen before. Media Molecule, the creators of the LittleBigPlanet series, set out to build an environment that players would want to be a part of and build on. Literally. There's a main adventure for players to conquer, but the best part is the series' revolutionary editor-mode that players can use on the world or the characters themselves. The main characters are small floppy creatures known as Sackpeople. Players can choose between Sackboy and Sackgirl and customize them with everything from Afros to zebra skin.

LittleBigPlanet is a 2.5D platformer, meaning all the visuals are 3D, but players can only move in a set path from side to side. The series added a clever twist to this concept by letting Sackpeople jump between the foreground and the background of environments. It can be a bit tricky, but it makes the game's prominent physics-based puzzles even more fun. And finally, you can get crafty and not have to worry about getting glitter all over!

DID YOU KNOW?
In the prototype for LittleBigPlanet, Sackboy was originally a blocky 2D character known as Mr. Yellowhead.

Played it! ☐ My Rating: ☆☆☆☆☆
My Favorite Moment: _____
Notes: _____
_____

TEARAWAY

The PlayStation Vita may not be the bestselling handheld of all time, but this little gaming-device-that-could has found fans in every corner of the globe. One of the Vita's first titles to really win players over was 3D platformer *Tearaway*. The game was lovingly crafted by Media Molecule, the developers behind the monster PlayStation hit *LittleBigPlanet*.

The games use cameras to make players part of the action in subtle ways, such as making their faces the center of the shining sun in the sky. The narrators even reference the player, known as "the you," when they're guiding the main characters on their journey. Not to be outdone by their predecessor, *Tearaway* lets players design small aspects of the world around them as the game progresses. Players might be asked to make a crown for a squirrel, a snowflake for a blizzard, or even a new eyeball for their own character. Personal touches, fantastic visuals, and top-notch gameplay make *Tearaway* a must-play for anyone who wants to think outside of the box—not to mention play as a character who could be made out of a box.

DID YOU KNOW?

The female protagonist ATOI gets her name from the French "*À toi*," which means "to you," a fitting name for someone trying to deliver a special message.

PLAY IT ON:
PS4 and PSVita

GENRE:
Platformer

RATING:
E

FIRST SEEN:
2013

MADE BY:
Media Molecule

Played it! ☐   My Rating: ☆☆☆☆☆
My Favorite Moment: _____
Notes: _____
_____

15

MEGA MAN

The year is 20XX. Robots are used to help the citizens of the world, until the diabolical Dr. Wiley decides to turn them against humanity. Wiley's former partner Dr. Light has no choice but to send his android sidekick, Mega Man, out to face the tough-as-nails robot masters that have conquered the world.

PLAY IT ON:
PS4, XOne, 3DS, and more

GENRE:
Platformer

RATING:
E

FIRST SEEN:
1987

MADE BY:
Capcom

DID YOU KNOW?
Mega Man is known as Rockman in Japan. He also has a robotic sister whose name is Roll. Get it? Rock and Roll!

The Mega Man franchise was first introduced in the late '80s and was a smash hit on the original NES. Each game featured the humanoid robot Mega Man using his trusty Mega Buster to take down new gangs of robot masters crafted by Dr. Wiley. The series is known for featuring some super offbeat bosses such as Wood Man, Dust Man, and Clown Man. Upon defeating the bosses, Mega Man obtains each of their signature attacks and can use them to take down future robotic menaces. In the end, players always have to catch up to Dr. Wiley and put him in his place once again.

Since *Mega Man 8* came out in 1996, it took over 12 years for *Mega Man 9* to finally see the light of day. Both *Mega Man 9* and *10* were created as digital-only games that players could download for PlayStation 3, Wii, or Xbox 360. Despite being released on powerful modern consoles, the games kept the 8-bit look of the original series. Recently, Capcom released the *Mega Man Legacy Collection*, a game that included the first six Mega Man titles, as well as a museum of never-before-seen concept art and an all-new challenge mode. Any platforming fans should give it a shot!

WHAT TO PLAY NEXT:
The Mega Man X series
The Azure Striker Gunvolt series
Shovel Knight

TOP SERIES PICKS:
Mega Man 2 (NES, 1989)
Mega Man 3 (NES, 1990)
Mega Man 9 (Wii, PS3, X360, 2008)

YOU'LL LIKE THESE GAMES IF...
Your favorite dance move is The Robot.

Played it! ☐   My Rating: ☆☆☆☆☆
My Favorite Moment: _____
Notes: _____
_____

16

MEGA MAN X

PLAY IT ON:
Wii U, 3DS,
SNES, and more

GENRE:
Platformer

RATING:
E

**FIRST
SEEN:**
1993

MADE BY:
Capcom

In the even-more-distant future, a group of robots with free will join together under the watchful eyes of a villain named Sigma. Each of Sigma's robotic armies are headed by leaders known as Mavericks. Dr. Light, the creator of the original Mega Man, wakes his newest creation to bring hope to the world once more, this time in the form of Mega Man X!

The Mega Man X games follow many of the same gameplay aspects the initial Mega Man series featured, but this time around, our hero, usually just called X, is taller, sleeker, and packing even more firepower under the hood. Players can upgrade his armor, life bar, and more by defeating bosses and seeking out hidden rooms. Unlike the robot masters of the original series, Mega Man X titles feature bosses that are almost all based on animals. These enhanced mechanical foes include the likes of Blizzard Buffalo, Overdrive Ostrich, Flame Mammoth, and dozens more. Once defeated, X gains their powers as his own and can move on to defeat Sigma.

While there hasn't been an entry in the series for a while, many of the games can be found on the Nintendo virtual console. Just remember—X marks the spot!

DID YOU KNOW?
All the bosses in the English version of *Mega Man X5* are named after members of rock band Guns N' Roses.

Played it! ☐ My Rating: ☆☆☆☆☆

My Favorite Moment: _____

Notes: _____

_____

RAYMAN

Rayman est une magnifique série de jeux vidéo! That's French for, "Rayman is a magnificent video-game series," fitting introduction for one of the most famous game characters to ever come from France.

Rayman's gaming debut focused on skillfully animated 2D platforming and unique character movement. The game features bizarre worlds, like the musical Band Land and the tasty Candy Château, that go hand in hand with the funky hero developers brought to life. Rayman has no arms or legs, yet he has hands and feet. He's not necessarily a human, but he's not really an animal either. Rayman is… different. But in all the right ways! His lack of arms gives him the ability to literally throw punches from far away, while his spiky hair can be used as a propeller to reach greater heights.

After taking a break from his 2D adventures and getting into some 3D mischief, Rayman returned to the world of side-scrolling platformers with *Rayman Origins*, which launched in 2011. The title uses a special game engine that lets developers focus on the art of the game and make animations flow like a cartoon. The sequel, *Rayman Legends,* was released not long after to rave reviews. Who needs arms and legs anyway?

DID YOU KNOW?

When developers first tried to render Rayman fighting and jumping, they couldn't get his arms or legs quite right, so they left them off. Eventually, they realized they liked his lack of limbs and went with that.

PLAY IT ON:
Switch, PS4, XOne, and more

GENRE:
Platformer

RATING:
E–E10+

FIRST SEEN:
1995

MADE BY:
Ubisoft

Played it! ☐ My Rating: ☆☆☆☆☆

My Favorite Moment: _____

Notes: _____

_____

18

SONIC

PLAY IT ON:
Switch, PS4,
XOne, and more

GENRE:
Platformer

RATING:
E–E10+

FIRST SEEN:
1991

MADE BY:
SEGA

Back in the early '90s, the SEGA Genesis wasn't doing so hot in the fight against Nintendo's entertainment systems. SEGA needed a mascot that would appeal to a new audience of older kids and teenagers. After a few failed attempts, the folks at SEGA started on Project Needlemouse, a game starring a hedgehog (then named Mr. Needlemouse) who was all about two things: speed and attitude. After many redesigns, Sonic the Hedgehog was born. He was promoted as a rival to Mario, the mascot of SEGA's main competitor, Nintendo.

Sonic's gameplay was so fresh and fast that the Genesis soon jumped to the top of the gaming sales charts, leaving Mario momentarily in the dust. The original title features Sonic running quickly and bopping foes as he makes his way through loops and across brightly colored worlds. His goal is always to take down the evil Dr. Robotnik (now known as Dr. Eggman) and save the day. The original Sonic was followed up by many 16-bit sequels that introduced his flying-fox sidekick, Tails, and improved the blue blur's speedy abilities. Much like Mario and other 2D heroes, Sonic eventually made the transition to 3D platforming games with titles like *Sonic 3D Blast* (SEGA Saturn) and *Sonic Adventures* (Dreamcast), proving that he could still push the limits of speed even in the 3D world.

SEGA eventually stopped making consoles, but they continued to make Sonic games for other systems. Today Sonic can be found on just about every console and handheld—even Nintendo ones! In fact, Sonic and Mario have teamed up on multiple occasions to compete in Olympic events and duke it out in the Super Smash Bros. series. Gotta go fast!

DID YOU KNOW?

In 1993, Sonic became the first gaming mascot to get its own balloon in the famous Macy's Thanksgiving Day Parade. Sonic may have been going too fast though, as his balloon hit a street lamp and popped before the parade was over!

WHAT TO PLAY NEXT:

The Super Mario Bros. series
Rayman Legends
Freedom Planet

TOP SERIES PICKS:

Sonic the Hedgehog 3 (GEN, 1994)
Sonic Adventures 2 (DC, 2001)
Sonic Mania (Switch, PS4, XOne,
PC, 2017)

YOU'LL LIKE THESE GAMES IF...

You feel the need for speed!

Played it! ☐   My Rating: ☆☆☆☆☆

My Favorite Moment: _____

Notes: _____

_____

19

SUPER MONKEY BALL

PLAY IT ON:
PSVita, 3DS, GC,
and more

GENRE:
Platformer

RATING:
E

**FIRST
SEEN:**
2001

MADE BY:
SEGA

After years of battling head-to-head with mascots like Mario and Sonic, SEGA and Nintendo finally teamed up. In 2001, SEGA agreed to bring their new arcade-platformer series to Nintendo's newest console, the GameCube. Thus the world was introduced to *Super Monkey Ball*, the first SEGA game to ever grace a Nintendo system.

The controls to *Super Monkey Ball* are absolutely bananas. While it may look like players are controlling the various monkeys, they're actually controlling the level as a whole. Imagine picking up a plate with a marble on it. To move the marble, you tilt the plate. That's how *Super Monkey Ball* works—players tilt the levels to roll their primates to the final goal. It takes some getting used to, but once players have it down, they can speed through dangerous sections and over tricky obstacles with ease. Players have the option of playing as four different monkeys (AiAi, MeeMee, Baby, and GonGon), and increasing difficulty settings. It's a fantastic series to play with friends and family, as players race, fight, and even go bowling with their favorite monkeys. Everyone is sure to have a ball!

DID YOU KNOW?

Super Monkey Ball's original release was a Japan-only arcade machine with a joystick that looked like a real banana.

Played it! ☐   My Rating: ☆☆☆☆☆

My Favorite Moment: _____

Notes: _____

_____

SHANTAE

Husband-and-wife team Matt and Erin Bozon came up with the concept for Shantae way back in 1994. Erin envisioned the main heroine, while Matt focused on building the world around her. The two worked tirelessly on the first game, known simply as *Shantae*. It was a hit with players and critics, but the game sold poorly because it came out for the Game Boy Color and not the newer Game Boy Advance.

Shantae soon gained a cult following, and players were finally treated to a sequel eight years later. With even more fans in tow, more Shantae games were produced. The most recent title, *½ Genie Hero*, was even crowdfunded by fans who were happy to pitch in to pay for the development of a new game.

Shantae games focus on the main hero's quest to save Sequin Land from the dastardly clutches of the lady pirate Risky Boots. In many games, Shantae is tasked with finding mystical items, such as magic seals and elemental stones. The spirited half-genie uses her hair as a whip to take down magical foes and can even use her stylish dancing ability to transform into various creatures or teleport. Warning: Players may find their own dance moves do not produce the same results.

DID YOU KNOW?

Shantae's long and powerful hair is based on creator Erin Bozon's hair, which was once nine feet long!

PLAY IT ON:
PS4, XOne, Switch, and more

GENRE:
Platformer

RATING:
E–T

FIRST SEEN:
2002

MADE BY:
WayForward

Played it! ☐   My Rating: ☆☆☆☆☆
My Favorite Moment: _____
Notes: _____
_____

21

SKYLANDERS

If you've ever looked at your toys and wished they could join you on a grand adventure, then Skylanders is your kind of series. The games feature dozens of real-world figures for players to collect and use to unlock digital

PLAY IT ON:
PS4, XOne,
Switch, and more

GENRE:
Platformer

RATING:
E 10+

**FIRST
SEEN:**
2011

MADE BY:
Activision

DID YOU KNOW?
Donkey Kong, Bowser, and Crash Bandicoot have all guest starred
as playable characters in the Skylanders series.

characters in the main games. When the figures are placed on the Skylanders portal, they're transported to the Skylands, a world of floating islands and fantastical creatures.

Each new Skylanders title comes with a brand new twist that pulls players into the wacky world of the Skylands. There have been giants, traps, switchable body parts, vehicles, and more since the series launched in 2011. In *Skylanders Imaginators*, players are able to create their very own heroes, with the ability to customize their character's appearance, powers, weapons, and loads of other details.

The Skylanders are a legendary group of heroes that must use their elemental powers to stop the evil Kaos from taking over the Skylands and its surrounding worlds. To do this, the Skylanders have to battle their way across different realms, increasing their powers, solving puzzles, and defeating mighty opponents. Each Skylander is represented by a unique element, including fire, water, earth, air, magic, and more. These elemental powers give the Skylanders special attacks and access to certain parts of the Skylands that others may not be able to reach. This is where you, The Portal Master, come in! By switching which Skylander you have on the portal, you can bring a whole new element into play. The more Skylanders you have, the bigger the adventure!

WHAT TO PLAY NEXT:
The LEGO Dimensions series
The Disney Infinity series
The Spyro series

TOP SERIES PICKS:
Skylanders Swap Force (Wii U, PS4, XOne, and more, 2013)
Skylanders Superchargers (Wii U, PS4, XOne, and more, 2015)
Skylanders Imaginators (Wii U, PS4, XOne, and more, 2016)

YOU'LL LIKE THESE GAMES IF...
You have a crazy imagination.

Played it! ☐   My Rating: ☆☆☆☆☆

My Favorite Moment: _____

Notes: _____

_____

22

PSYCHONAUTS

PLAY IT ON:
PS4, PS3, PC
and more

GENRE:
Platformer

RATING:
T

**FIRST
SEEN:**
2005

MADE BY:
Double Fine
Productions

Welcome to Whispering Rock Psychic Summer Camp, the only summer camp that's not-so-secretly a government training facility for youngsters with psychic powers. You can enjoy a variety of activities, including mental canoeing, Psitanium arrowhead collecting, and battling cougars that can light you on fire with their minds. Actually, you might want to stay away from that last one…

Psychonauts follows the talented psychic Razputin, a former circus performer who sneaks into Camp Whispering Rock to hide from his disapproving father. He's only at the camp for a short time when he learns the terrible visions he's been having are coming true—the brains of other campers are being stolen! It's up to Raz to infiltrate the minds of the camp counselors and help his fellow campers save the day. As players progress through the game, they earn spiffy new merit badges that unlock Raz's psychic abilities, including invisibility and levitation.

The game is known for its bizarre characters and hilarious story, as well as some of the best platforming to come out of the PS2 era. Do you have the brains to take on an adventure that goes this deep?

DID YOU KNOW?
To make the *Psychonauts'* characters seem real, creator Tim Schafer made social-media accounts for each character.

Played it! ☐ My Rating: ☆☆☆☆☆

My Favorite Moment: _____

Notes: _____

_____

SHOVEL KNIGHT

Players who want a new way to experience the pretty pixels and iconic chiptune music of the original Nintendo should cast their gaze upon *Shovel Knight*. First-time developers Yacht Club Games were inspired by NES classics, such as *Mega Man, Zelda II*, and *Castlevania*. Their goal was to combine the best of the 8-bit era into one silly adventure, and it's safe to say they succeeded.

The retro-style game puts players in the shoes of the noble Shovel Knight, a hero on a quest to save his partner, Shield Knight, from the wicked Enchantress. On his journey to the fabled Tower of Fate, Shovel Knight must defeat The Order of No Quarter, a band of notorious knights who are determined to stop him. Players can use the treasure they uncover to upgrade Shovel Knight with stronger armor, new weapons, and even more powerful shovels. Of course, Shovel Knight fights for more than chivalry. He fights for shovelry!

Since launching the initial *Shovel Knight* title, the fine folks at Yacht Club Games have created two new adventure campaigns starring former villains Plague Knight and Specter Knight. A Shovel Knight amiibo figure and a two-player mode have also been released. Can you dig it?

PLAY IT ON:
Switch, 3DS, PS4, and more

GENRE:
Platformer

RATING:
E

FIRST SEEN:
2014

MADE BY:
Yacht Club Games

DID YOU KNOW?

In 2013, Yacht Club Games used the crowdfunding website Kickstarter to fund *Shovel Knight*. They ended up raising $311,502—an astounding 400% of their original goal!

Played it! ☐   My Rating: ☆☆☆☆☆
My Favorite Moment: _____
Notes: _____
_____

24

THE LEGEND OF ZELDA

PLAY IT ON:
Switch, Wii U,
3DS, and more

GENRE:
Action &
Adventure

RATING:
E–T

**FIRST
SEEN:**
1986

MADE BY:
Nintendo

With a title like *The Legend of Zelda*, you might think the hero of this series is Zelda. But turn on the game, and you'll find yourself face-to-face with elfin Link, a green-clad warrior with pointy ears and a long stocking cap. Despite Princess Zelda's major role in many of the critically acclaimed games, she's rarely a playable character in Link's many adventures. And only Link can bring peace back to a land overrun by the beast Ganon!

The Zelda series was created by master game designer Shigeru Miyamoto, father of Mario, Donkey Kong, Star Fox, and many other classics. Miyamoto's childhood exploits in the countryside of Kyoto, Japan, inspired the first Zelda title. Because he wanted players to feel the thrill of discovering hidden secrets and venturing into mysterious places, the original *The Legend of Zelda* invites players to explore a huge fantasy world called Hyrule as they quest for the eight pieces of the fabled Triforce. All Zelda titles follow a similar path, with players solving puzzles and acquiring items along their journey to save the land from an encroaching evil. Though every protagonist in the Zelda series appears to be the same elfish hero, most are actually hundreds of years apart on the game's sprawling timeline. (Is it any wonder Link is commonly referred to as The Hero of Time?)

When the game launched in North America, it featured an extraordinary golden cartridge that players still seek out today. In recent years, Nintendo has remade many of the best-selling Zelda titles for their new systems, including *Ocarina of Time* and *Majora's Mask* for the 3DS, as well as *The Wind Waker* and *Twilight Princess* for Wii U. The newest Zelda game, *Breath of the Wild* was one of the last games for the Wii U and one of the first for the Nintendo Switch.

DID YOU KNOW?

The Legend of Zelda for NES was the first console video game that allowed players to save their progress. Other games required players to input codes or simply start from the beginning every time they played.

WHAT TO PLAY NEXT:
Ōkami
*Oceanhorn: Monster of the
Uncharted Seas*
Hyrule Warriors

TOP SERIES PICKS:
*The Legend of Zelda: A Link to the
Past* (SNES, 1991)
*The Legend of Zelda: Ocarina of
Time 3D* (3DS, 2011)
*The Legend of Zelda: Breath of the
Wild* (Switch, Wii U, 2017)

YOU'LL LIKE THESE GAMES IF...
You have a lot of heart!

Played it! ☐　My Rating: ☆☆☆☆☆

My Favorite Moment: _____

Notes: _____

_____

25

METROID

PLAY IT ON:
3DS, Wii U, Wii,
and more

GENRE:
Action &
Adventure

RATING:
E–T

**FIRST
SEEN:**
1986

MADE BY:
Nintendo

When the first Metroid game was released in 1986, it carried with it an amazing secret. The main protagonist, laser-cannon-wielding Samus Aran, was… a woman! This may not seem like a big deal to gamers today, but there weren't many female video-game heroes at the time. Players learned the truth when they completed the game, so even after the launch, many Nintendo fans were unaware that one of the universe's greatest bounty hunters was indeed a woman.

DID YOU KNOW?

Samus Aran's last name was taken from famous soccer player Pelé, whose real name is Edson Arantes do Nascimento.

The original Metroid games are a mix of the Super Mario Bros. and The Legend of Zelda series. They feature platforming, but also encourage players to explore large worlds in search of new weapons and clues. The story focuses on Samus Aran and her adventures to stop the fiendish Space Pirates from stealing the power of parasitic aliens known as Metroid. Samus must blast her way through hordes of otherworldly opponents and brave the depths of mysterious planets, such as Zebus and the Metroid home world SR388, to ensure the pirates don't get their mitts on any of the coveted aliens. Players can upgrade Samus' abilities as they go, enhancing her power suit with new energy beams and armor. Samus is also known for rolling into a "morph ball" to fit in tight spaces and lay land mines.

In 2002, after an eight-year break, Samus made the jump to first-person view with the launch of *Metroid Prime*. Players could finally see through Samus' eyes and experience the world of Metroid in 3D for the first time. *Metroid Prime's* two sequels became bestselling titles for the GameCube and Wii, further cementing Samus' legacy as one of gaming's greatest characters.

WHAT TO PLAY NEXT:
Guacamelee!
Cave Story
Ori and the Blind Forest

TOP SERIES PICKS:
Super Metroid (SNES, 1994)
Metroid Fusion (GBA, 2002)
Metroid Prime: Trilogy (Wii, 2009)

YOU'LL LIKE THESE GAMES IF...
You think laser cannons are a blast.

Played it! ☐ My Rating: ☆☆☆☆☆
My Favorite Moment: _____
Notes: _____
_____

26

CAVE STORY

PLAY IT ON:
Switch, 3DS, PC,
and more

GENRE:
Action &
Adventure

RATING:
E10+

**FIRST
SEEN:**
2004

MADE BY:
Studio Pixel

For five years, Daisuke "Pixel" Amaya quietly built every element of the game known in English as *Cave Story*. Slowly but surely, he compiled the music, characters, story, and gameplay mechanics into one epic, retro adventure. When it was finally done, Amaya released the game as freeware, meaning it could be downloaded by anyone at no cost.

The game focuses on a nameless hero who awakens deep in an underground village with no recollection of who he is or how he came to be there. Within the village, players learn of the Mimigas, a race of bunny-like people who are being harassed by someone called The Doctor. It's up to our nameless character to protect the people of this world and decipher his own past. The gameplay is similar to series like Metroid, where players gain upgrades to their weapons and health along the journey.

Upon its release, *Cave Story* became one of the most downloaded freeware games on the web, and full-time gaming companies took notice. Enhanced versions of *Cave Story* have been released on PC, Wii, and more, usually under the title *Cave Story+*. A reworked 3D version of the game was also produced in 2011 for the 3DS. It's a true fave story!

DID YOU KNOW?
Many of the original enemies in *Cave Story* were designed after bars of soap.

Played it! ☐   My Rating: ☆☆☆☆☆
My Favorite Moment: _____
Notes: _____

_____

JOURNEY

If anyone ever asks if you've heard of "Thatgamecompany," they aren't being forgetful. The studio Thatgamecompany is world renowned for producing visually stunning and meaningful games that anyone can enjoy. Their greatest game to date is the descriptively titled *Journey*, which puts players in the shoes of a red-robed desert wanderer who's attempting to reach a far-off mountain. Players must guide the robed figure through various environments, learning about the character's past by observing ancient murals and long-forgotten structures. The game is unique for many reasons, including the fact that there isn't a single word spoken throughout the entire adventure—a feature that's especially strange considering the game is played online with others. Players can produce small "chirps" to alert an ally, but there is no direct communication between players and no way to know who you're playing with, even as you progress through the story side by side. Names and talking are unnecessary. All that really matters is sharing the adventure together.

Journey is a short yet emotionally charged experience. Players will find themselves falling in love with the combination of staggering visuals and moving music as they make their pilgrimage to the glowing mountain peak in the distance. Will you complete the journey?

PLAY IT ON:
PS4 and PS3

GENRE:
Action &
Adventure

RATING:
E

**FIRST
SEEN:**
2012

DID YOU KNOW?

The soundtrack for *Journey* was the first video-game score to receive a Grammy Award nomination.

MADE BY:
Thatgamecompany

Played it! ☐   My Rating: ☆☆☆☆☆
My Favorite Moment: _____
Notes: _____
_____

28

ŌKAMI

PLAY IT ON:
PS3, PS2, and DS

GENRE:
Action &
Adventure

RATING:
E10+–T

**FIRST
SEEN:**
2006

MADE BY:
Capcom

Japan, often referred to as *The Land of the Rising Sun*, is a country with a rich and varied mythology. Folklore and ancient tales have been passed down from generation to generation through spoken stories and books. Now that tradition continues with the world of video games. The Ōkami series is one of the best games to use legendary historical influences to drive its story and characters.

DID YOU KNOW?
The word *Ōkami* means "wolf" in Japanese, but it's also a play on *kami* which means "god." A perfect match for a game about a wolf goddess!

The original *Ōkami* is about a sun goddess named Amaterasu, who takes the form of a white wolf. Amaterasu (nicknamed Ammy) is accompanied by Issun, a wandering artist who just so happens to be a flea. As Ammy cannot speak, Issun often speaks on her behalf, making jokes and helping players move on to the next task. The unlikely pair are hot on the trail of Orochi, an eight-headed demon who has cursed the land of Nippon.

What really sets *Ōkami* apart is its whimsical art style, which is based on classic Japanese ink-wash paintings. Players even get to test their hands at the ancient art form by using Ammy's Celestial Brush technique. With this power, players can momentarily pause the action and draw on the screen in different patterns. By battling new enemies and lifting the curse upon the land, players learn new brushstrokes to grow trees, slash baddies, and even make the sun rise.

In 2010, a long-awaited sequel to *Ōkami* was released for the Nintendo DS. It starred one of Amaterasu's pups and included more of the original's revolutionary brush techniques, this time using the touch screen of the DS. The whole series is truly a work of art.

WHAT TO PLAY NEXT:
The Legend of Zelda series
ICO
Shadow of the Colossus

TOP SERIES PICKS:
Ōkami (PS2, 2006)
Ōkamiden (DS, 2010)
Ōkami HD (PS3, 2012)

YOU'LL LIKE THESE GAMES IF...
You're an artist at heart.

Played it! ☐   My Rating: ☆☆☆☆☆
My Favorite Moment: _____
Notes: _____
_____

29

BOMBERMAN

PLAY IT ON:
Switch, iOS,
SNES, and more

GENRE:
Action &
Adventure

RATING:
E–T

**FIRST
SEEN:**
1983

MADE BY:
Hudson Soft

You may have heard of Mega Man or Rayman, but how about Bomberman? The bomb-tossing hero has been blowing up friends and enemies alike for over 30 years. Though the main character is known for his white jumpsuit, over the years, a rainbow of other Bombermen have been introduced for players to control.

Bomberman is traditionally played from a top-down view with players trapped in a maze of walls. Bombs can be used to blow up obstacles, including any opponents who dare cross Bomberman's path. To win the round, players must clear the area. Later games introduce bombs that are more powerful, as well as ones that blow up with a special elemental explosion.

Part of the fun of playing this game is sharing the experience with friends. In *Bomberman* released for the TurboGrafx system in 1991, groups of up to five people could compete against each other using a device called the TurboTap. *Super Bomberman*, which launched for the Super Nintendo in 1993, followed suit by letting players use a multi-tap that allows up to four people to compete. With its simple yet strategic gameplay, the Bomberman series is truly a blast to play!

DID YOU KNOW?

Bomberman's second title, *3D Bomberman*, was exclusive to Japan and the only game in the series to feature a first-person view.

Played it! ☐ My Rating: ☆☆☆☆☆

My Favorite Moment: _____

Notes: _____

_____

GUACAMELEE!

30

Games like *Ōkami* (#28 on our list) show that video games can find some seriously awesome inspiration in the customs and folklore of ancient cultures. *Guacamelee!* includes bits of Mexican tradition in its story line, while poking fun at the world of gaming along the way. The colorful world of luchador wrestling is on full display, and players are in for an extraordinary, otherworldly adventure.

When Mexican farmer Juan attempts to rescue his love from the clutches of the evil skeleton Carlos Calaca, he soon finds himself in the land of the dead. Juan is given a second chance at life when the mystical luchador Tostada presents him with a legendary wrestling mask. Juan is transformed into a powerful luchador and heads back to the land of the living to seek revenge on Carlos and his army of supernatural evildoers.

As in series like Metroid and Cave Story, players must navigate long, maze-like environments filled with lurking enemies and puzzles to solve. While most games have players upgrade their weapons, *Guacamelee!* stands apart with its arsenal of powerful hand-to-hand attacks. Players learn to headbutt skeletons, body slam ancient monsters, and more. It's all in a day's work for Juan, the luchador with nerves of steel and a flaming uppercut.

DID YOU KNOW?

Posters in the background of certain levels feature wrestling versions of favorite video game characters, including Los Super Hermanos (Super Mario Bros.)!

PLAY IT ON:
Wii U, PS4, XOne, and more

GENRE:
Action & Adventure

RATING:
E10+

FIRST SEEN:
2013

MADE BY:
DrinkBox Studios

Played it! ☐ My Rating: ☆☆☆☆☆
My Favorite Moment: _____
Notes: _____

31

LEGO DIMENSIONS

PLAY IT ON:
PS4, XOne, Wii U,
and more

GENRE:
Action &
Adventure

RATING:
E 10+

**FIRST
SEEN:**
2015

MADE BY:
TT Games

Imagination is a powerful tool that lets you bring your favorite toys and playthings to life. *LEGO Dimensions* makes this idea a reality, letting players open a portal into a world of shiny bricks and master builders. The coolest part about this toys-to-life series is that all the mini-figures and sets are based on real LEGO pieces that can be used outside the game.

DID YOU KNOW?
One level pack houses many of Midway Arcade's classic 8-bit games. Players can install it to play a video game inside a video game!

The story of *LEGO Dimensions* focuses on three heroes: Batman (DC Comics), Gandalf (Lord of the Rings), and Wyldstyle (*The LEGO Movie*). After attempting to rescue their friends from a mysterious vortex, the three LEGO legends are accidentally warped to the planet Vorton. It is here that they learn the villainous Lord Vortech has been wreaking havoc on the LEGO Multiverse so he can acquire the twelve Foundation Elements and take the multiverse as his own. Players guide Batman, Gandalf, and Wyldstyle through various LEGO worlds, including famous franchises like Ghostbusters, Scooby-Doo, Doctor Who, and Back to the Future. The *LEGO Dimensions* starter set comes with physical versions of the three main heroes, as well as a huge interactive LEGO portal for players to build. Fans of the game can buy extra characters and level packs, play as their favorite mini-figures, and unlock special vehicles along the way.

Unlike many series, *LEGO Dimensions* only has one main game that's updated with new levels and characters as time goes on. The portal and game disc that launched with the game in 2015 can still be used today with new and upcoming sets like Sonic, Fantastic Beasts, Teen Titans Go!, and more. The best part is that players don't necessarily need all the sets to complete the game's main adventure. Better get building!

WHAT TO PLAY NEXT:
The LEGO Star Wars series
The LEGO Harry Potter series
The Skylanders series

TOP LEVEL PACK PICKS:
The Simpsons Level Pack
Portal 2 Level Pack
Adventure Time Level Pack

YOU'LL LIKE THESE GAMES IF...
You're a master builder.

Played it! ☐   My Rating: ☆☆☆☆☆

My Favorite Moment: _____

Notes: _____

_____

32

APE ESCAPE

PLAY IT ON:
PS4, PSVita, PS,
and more

GENRE:
Action &
Adventure

RATING:
E–T

**FIRST
SEEN:**
1999

MADE BY:
Sony
Interactive
Entertainment

Each primate in the Ape Escape series wears a special Peak Point Helmet that makes it extra clever and terribly mischievous. Where would a monkey get such a device? The answer lies with the monkey Specter, the original test subject of the mind-altering helmet. When his own helmet goes haywire, he upgrades every monkey helmet he can get his hands on. The enhanced primates find their way to a nearby time machine and escape to different periods in time. It's up to the protagonist Spike and his friends to go after the monkeys and save history. He uses his trusty Time Net, a device that both captures and transports monkeys back to the current time. With his net and an arsenal of other gadgets, Spike must stun, trap, and capture the monkeys before they do too much damage.

Ape Escape was the first game specifically built to be played with the original PlayStation's DualShock controller. The controller featured two joysticks instead of the usual directional pad, giving players more movement and camera abilities. In the case of Ape Escape, a flick of the joystick swings nets and other gadgets that help players nab those pesky primates. Just watch out, because these monkeys are bananas!

DID YOU KNOW?
Despite the name, there are no actual apes in the Ape Escape series. All the escaped primates are said to be monkeys, which are scientifically different than apes.

Played it! ☐ My Rating: ☆☆☆☆☆
My Favorite Moment: _____
Notes: _____

LUIGI'S MANSION

There's nothing scarier than living in the shadow of your older sibling's success. Well, maybe a haunted mansion full of ghosts is scarier. And poor Luigi is forced to face both these horrors in his very own spooky adventure series!

Though fans were used to seeing Luigi play second fiddle to his famous brother, Mario, in *Luigi's Mansion*, Mario is the one in need of rescuing after being captured and held prisoner in an otherworldly painting. Unlike classic Mushroom Kingdom outings, the Luigi's Mansion series is more of a perplexing puzzle than a fast-paced platformer. With the help of Professor E. Gadd, Luigi must exterminate the ghosts that imprisoned his brother, so he straps on the powerful Poltergust 3000, a vacuum that's specially designed to suck up spirits. Players can unlock new rooms and collect clues to Mario's whereabouts while exploring the mysterious mansion.

The second Luigi's Mansion came to the 3DS in 2013, a full 12 years after the first game. This time around, the trembling hero is faced with five different mansions. There's also a Luigi's Mansion arcade game that's found almost exclusively in Japan that features motion controls and a huge vacuum controller. It truly sucks—in a good way!

DID YOU KNOW?
A ghost called ComBooter in *Luigi's Mansion: Dark Moon* shouts, "01100010 01101111 01101111!" when you find him. That's binary for "boo!"

PLAY IT ON:
3DS, GC, and Arcade

GENRE:
Action & Adventure

RATING:
E

FIRST SEEN:
2001

MADE BY:
Nintendo

Played it! ☐ My Rating: ☆☆☆☆☆
My Favorite Moment: _____
Notes: _____

34

PLAY IT ON:
Switch and Wii U

GENRE:
Action &
Adventure

RATING:
E 10+

**FIRST
SEEN:**
2015

MADE BY:
Nintendo

SPLATOON

Third-person shooter *Splatoon*, released for the Wii U in 2015, is Nintendo's biggest new franchise in recent years. The series focuses on Inklings, teenage squid-like creatures obsessed with fashion and battling for territory with their flashy ink attacks. Though the games feature many different modes, the most popular is known as Turf War. Players battle in teams of four to cover as much ground as possible with their squad's vibrant ink, while the opposing side does the same. When Inklings are wading through their own ink, they can momentarily transform into squids and swim about

to gain speed or hide from foes. Loads of paint-spewing weapons are at the Inklings' disposal, including giant paint rollers, long-range charge shots, splat bombs, and more. Each weapon comes with a special attack that can deliver a devastating blow to the other team. Inkling fashion also plays a big part in the game's battles—certain gear can give players stat boosts for abilities—such as faster ink recovery and increased swim speed. The series' single-player adventures are definitely worth exploring, but the online multiplayer mode is where you'll find all the real action.

Splatoon 2, an exclusive on the Nintendo Switch, adds even more colorful firepower and radical squid style. Better suit up, because things are about to get messy.

WHAT TO PLAY NEXT:
Super Mario Sunshine
De Blob
Paper Mario Color Splash

TOP SERIES PICKS:
Splatoon
Splatoon 2

DID YOU KNOW?
Early prototypes for *Splatoon* featured humans, rabbits, and even giant blocks of tofu battling over turf.

YOU'LL LIKE THESE GAMES IF...
You're a squid or a kid.

Played it! ☐ My Rating: ☆☆☆☆☆
My Favorite Moment: _____
Notes: _____

35

THE LAST GUARDIAN

PLAY IT ON:
PS4

GENRE:
Action &
Adventure

RATING:
T

**FIRST
SEEN:**
2016

MADE BY:
SIE Japan

Over the years, Team ICO, a part of Sony's Interactive Entertainment Japan Studio, has become famous for churning out legendary titles that players rank among the top in gaming history. The team is named after their first game *ICO*, a fan-favorite PlayStation 2 adventure. Their second title, *Shadow of the Colossus*, was an even bigger hit and is widely considered one of the best games ever made.

For their third masterpiece, Team ICO created *The Last Guardian*, the story of a boy and his enormous animal companion. The boy, who is never given a name, is kidnapped for unknown reasons and wakes to find himself covered in tattoos and being held prisoner. Soon he comes face-to-face with a giant feathered creature that resembles a griffin (a mythical creature that's half-lion and half-eagle). The two must kindle their friendship, help each other escape from the mysterious prison, and find the evil responsible for bringing them there.

Like *ICO* and *Shadow of the Colossus*, *The Last Guardian* won fans and critics over with the relationships between the characters, beautiful art direction, and powerful soundtrack. If you've ever had an animal friend, you'll surely understand the connection between the main character and his lovable beast.

DID YOU KNOW?

A trailer for *The Last Guardian* was released in 2009 and showed the game as a PlayStation 3 exclusive, but the game didn't come out for another seven years and ended up on the more powerful PlayStation 4.

Played it! ☐   My Rating: ☆☆☆☆☆
My Favorite Moment: _____
Notes: _____
_____

JET SET RADIO

Do you like funky hip-hop beats and street-wise skaters? If so, then the Jet Set Radio series just might be your jam. The iconic SEGA franchise is well known for its unique urban atmosphere and upbeat characters.

Set within popular real-world locations in Tokyo, the game follows a gang of skaters and artists who call themselves the GGs. Beat, the lanky front man, is joined by his friends Gum and Tab. Together they use spray paint to tag their territory and rebel against corporations. When other gangs step in on their turf, it's up to the GGs to grind and spray their way back to the top of the streets. The game's nearly weightless jumps and wall rides let players take their skaters to new heights and find even more territory to claim.

The soundtrack for the Jet Set Radio series is regarded as one of the best in gaming history, with each main release region (Japan, North America, and Europe) receiving its own special tracks.

Just remember, in the real world, spray painting or tagging property that doesn't belong to you is against the law. So be smart about where you put your art.

PLAY IT ON:
PS3, PC, DC, and more

GENRE:
Action & Adventure

RATING:
T

FIRST SEEN:
2000

DID YOU KNOW?

On the pre-release European box art for *Jet Set Radio*, main character Beat was accidentally drawn with six fingers on one hand. Whoops!

MADE BY:
SEGA

Played it! ☐ My Rating: ☆☆☆☆☆

My Favorite Moment: _____

Notes: _____

_____

37

MINECRAFT

PLAY IT ON:
PC, Switch, PS4,
and more

GENRE:
Action &
Adventure

RATING:
E 10+

**FIRST
SEEN:**
2011

MADE BY:
Mojang

Minecraft drops players into a blocky world full of tools, elements, animals, and enemies. Players can break down or build up blocks in the game by mining different materials and combining them.

Minecraft has three main gameplay modes to choose from: Survival, Creative, and Adventure. In survival mode, players must brave the elements while fighting off randomly spawning monsters (and hunger!). Players can build weapons, shelters, and hundreds of other items to weather the dangerous world filled with Creepers, Spiders, Ghasts, and a slew of monsters lurking in the dark. Creative mode is much more laid back—players have unlimited materials and the ability to build without worrying about monsters attacks. Players can even fly and admire their wondrous creations from the sky. Adventure mode lets players explore a world made by another Minecraft player.

One of the greatest parts of Minecraft is that you can build and quest for items with your friends! Collaborate with others to build amazing structures and fight off mobs of baddies with more firepower.

In 2015, Telltale Games released *Minecraft: Story Mode,* a point-and-click adventure set in the Minecraft world. Though it doesn't feature any actual building, the series does include all the materials, items, and opponents that players have grown to love. The game was released in eight episodes over a short period of time and eventually launched as *The Complete Collection* for multiple systems.

Since its release, Minecraft has sold over 100 million copies, making it the second best-selling video game of all time, behind the classic puzzle title *Tetris* (#79 on our list). In Minecraft, there is always something new to build, a new area to explore, and a new enemy to battle. With millions of options, the only limit is your imagination. So get building!

DID YOU KNOW?

Everyone's favorite enemy, the Creeper, was actually designed by accident when creator Markus Persson gave the wrong body proportions to a blocky pig. The upright design was later given a green texture and explosive abilities.

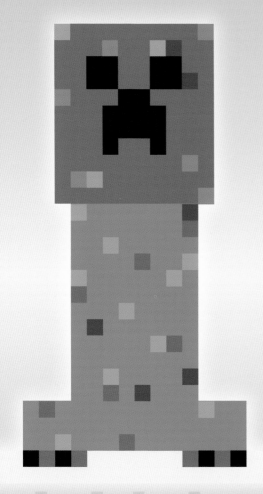

WHAT TO PLAY NEXT:
Terraria
Dragon Quest Builders
Super Mario Maker

TOP SERIES PICKS:
Minecraft (PC, 2011)
Minecraft: Pocket Edition
(iOS and Android, 2011)
Minecraft: Story Mode
(PC and more, 2015)

YOU'LL LIKE THESE GAMES IF...
You like to build with friends.

Played it! ☐   My Rating: ☆☆☆☆☆

My Favorite Moment: _____

Notes: _____

_____

38

TEENAGE MUTANT NINJA TURTLES

PLAY IT ON:
PS3, X360, SNES,
and more

GENRE:
Action &
Adventure

RATING:
E–T

FIRST SEEN:
1989

MADE BY:
Konami

Originally based on a gritty comic book in the mid '80s, the Teenage Mutant Ninja Turtles were adapted for TV and movies, and soon the Turtles were a household name. With radical heroes and plenty of ninja action, it was only a matter of time before the Turtles made the jump to gaming.

The story of the Ninja Turtles is set in New York City. The four reptile brothers find themselves transformed by a mysterious ooze that gives them and their rat caretaker, Master Splinter, humanoid bodies. The Turtles take the names Leonardo, Donatello, Raphael, and Michelangelo, and vow to help their master stop his former pupil, now known as the Shredder. Many people fear the Turtles' odd looks and ninja moves, but these awesome dudes are pretty much interested in only two things: saving the day and eating pizza.

Ready to try one of the many games in this series? The original 1989 arcade game and the Super Nintendo classic *Turtles in Time* were both released as side-scrolling beat'-em-ups that feature multiple players slowly making their way across levels as enemies jump out to attack, wave after wave, from off screen. Cowabunga, dude!

DID YOU KNOW?

The PC port of *Teenage Mutant Ninja Turtles* for the NES was literally unbeatable. When the developers reworked the game for PC, they made an important jump impossible to land.

Played it! ☐ My Rating: ☆☆☆☆☆

My Favorite Moment: _____

Notes: _____

_____

MONKEY ISLAND

Many modern adventure games involve fast-paced action and quick reflexes. But the Monkey Island series was designed as a point-and-click adventure, which requires more puzzle solving and creative thinking. Players are tasked with determining what to do next based on clues in the game. Created by gaming legend Ron Gilbert, the Monkey Island series stars Guybrush Threepwood, a bumbling wannabe pirate who falls head over heels for governor Elaine Marley while attempting to prove his worth. Unfortunately, the undead pirate LeChuck also has his eyes on Elaine and sends his army of skeletons to steal away Guybrush's beloved.

One of the best (and silliest) parts of Monkey Island is that instead of actually swinging blades at each other, the characters have rhyming "insult sword fights." You strike at your opponent with the best insult you can muster, and he retaliates with his most commendable comeback. When your opponent comes out swinging with, "You're the ugliest monster ever created!" all you need to do to take him down is answer with a snappy comeback. See, young pirates, there's never need for violence when you have a witty retort.

PLAY IT ON:
PC, iOS, PS3, and more

GENRE:
Action & Adventure

RATING:
E 10+

FIRST SEEN:
1990

MADE BY:
LucasArts

DID YOU KNOW?

Guybrush Threepwood's first name came from an art program where every file ended with ".brush" when saved. Guybrush was originally just a file named "guy.brush"!

Played it! ☐   My Rating: ☆☆☆☆☆
My Favorite Moment: _____
Notes: _____
_____

40

STAR FOX

PLAY IT ON:
Wii U, 3DS, N64, and more

GENRE:
Action & Adventure

RATING:
E–T

FIRST SEEN:
1993

MADE BY:
Nintendo

Outer space holds many mysteries. Where do black holes lead? Does life exist on other planets? Who gave a spaceship to a talking fox? Surprisingly, that last question has already been answered. The space epic known as Star Fox was created by Shigeru Miyamoto, the same genius developer

DID YOU KNOW?
If you type the famous *Star Fox 64* line, "Do a barrel roll," into the Google search engine and hit enter, the whole page will spin. Try it!

behind the Mario and Zelda series. The idea for the original *Star Fox* (released as *Starwing* in Europe) came from the Fushimi Inari shrine in Kyoto, Japan. The shrine has over 10,000 gates known as *torii* which inspired the many rings and gaps Fox must fly through while piloting his ship through space. The shrine is also home to dozens of fox statues (foxes are regarded as messengers for the ancient gods).

The Star Fox plot centers on Fox McCloud, a space pilot and leader of an ace animal crew that includes Peppy Hare (a rabbit), Falco Lombardi (a falcon) and Slippy Toad (you can figure that one out, right?). Team Star Fox is usually hot on the trail of the mad scientist Andross, who wants to rule the Lylat System and often shows up as a giant laser-shooting cyborg monkey head. The team is assisted by helpful allies, like the blue space fox Krystal and robot ROB 64.

Most of the games in the Star Fox series are categorized as on-the-rail shooters, meaning players can move around the screen as the level progresses, but can't go wherever they please. They must shoot down enemies and obstacles that fly into view while navigating the dangerous intergalactic territory. You'll only make it to the end with some fancy flying. Use the boost to get through!

WHAT TO PLAY NEXT:
Pokémon Snap
Rez Infinite
Sin and Punishment 2

TOP SERIES PICKS:
Star Fox (SNES, 1993)
Star Fox Assault (GC, 2002)
Star Fox 64 3D (3DS, 2011)

YOU'LL LIKE THESE GAMES IF...
You want to explore space.

Played it! ☐   My Rating: ☆☆☆☆☆
My Favorite Moment: _____
Notes: _____
_____

41

MARIO KART

PLAY IT ON:
Switch, Wii U,
3DS, and more

GENRE:
Sports &
Fighting

RATING:
E

**FIRST
SEEN:**
1992

MADE BY:
Nintendo

If the thought of a gorilla launching a flying, blue turtle shell at a princess—as both drift around the edge of a volcano in go-karts—sounds a bit ridiculous, you may not be ready for the Mario Kart series. The multiplayer kart-racing franchise has been around since the Super Nintendo days, and it still stands as one of the most popular and imitated racing games of all time.

DID YOU KNOW?

Nintendo teamed with Namco Bandai to create Mario Kart arcade games that include Pac-Man and other famous Namco Bandai characters as drivers.

The main Mario Kart racing campaign is known as the Grand Prix, and it consists of different competitive cups. Players can choose to race in different speed classes ranging from 50cc (the slowest) to 200cc (super fast). Each of the tracks in a cup has a different environment with obstacles to avoid and shortcuts to discover. The first player to cross the finish line is the winner, gaining points for the final standings and bragging rights until the next race.

While players race, they must swerve to hit boxes strategically placed throughout the track. Each box contains a random power-up for players to use to their advantage. There are slippery banana peels, engine-boosting mushrooms, a rainbow of dangerous turtle shells, and many other tricky power-ups that can boost your character to the front of the pack. These power-ups prove essential in Mario Kart's multiplayer battle mode, where players are dropped into an arena and must compete to be the last racer standing.

The Mario Kart roster of characters has grown with each game; the newest titles even feature racers from other Nintendo series, such as The Legend of Zelda, Splatoon, and Animal Crossing. Every character falls into a certain weight class and can be paired with a kart or bike that fits the player's racing style. Mushroom Kingdom racers, on your mark. Get set. GO!

WHAT TO PLAY NEXT:
Sonic & All-Stars Racing Transformed
Diddy Kong Racing
Crash Team Racing

TOP SERIES PICKS:
Mario Kart 64 (N64, 1996)
Mario Kart Double Dash!! (GC, 2003)
Mario Kart 8 Deluxe (Switch, 2017)

YOU'LL LIKE THESE GAMES IF...
Banana peels make you squeal.

Played it! ☐   My Rating: ☆☆☆☆☆
My Favorite Moment: _____
Notes: _____
_____

42

PUNCH-OUT!!

PLAY IT ON:
Wii U, Wii, SNES,
and more

GENRE:
Sports &
Fighting

RATING:
E–E10+

**FIRST
SEEN:**
1984

MADE BY:
Nintendo

After working on the Donkey Kong arcade game, Nintendo found itself with far too many video monitors at its Japanese headquarters. With so many extra screens lying around, the company challenged designers to come up with a game that used two screens instead of the usual one. The result was *Punch-Out!!*, a boxing game that showed player health and opponent stats on the top screen, while players duked it out on the bottom screen.

The original *Punch-Out!!* protagonist was a green, wire-frame boxer with no name. Since then, the main character has been Little Mac, a short powerhouse who likes to train in pink sweats. Players get to take swings at the most prestigious boxers in the Minor, Major, and World circuits, and each new formidable fighter has a unique backstory and boxing style.

While technically a sports-based franchise, Punch-Out!! games are all based on pattern recognition. Players must judge when and where to throw their punches while also dodging incoming blows and special attacks. Once players recognize an adversary's patterns, they can hit them where it hurts. It doesn't take much to knock Little Mac for a loop, so you'll have to be light on your feet and quick with a jab if you want to be champion!

DID YOU KNOW?

Many Nintendo characters can be found in the audience of *Punch-Out!!* games. In *Punch-Out!!* for Wii, players can even face off against Donkey Kong, who is the surprise final opponent in Last Stand mode.

Played it! ☐   My Rating: ☆☆☆☆☆
My Favorite Moment: _____
Notes: _____
_____

F-ZERO

When the Super Nintendo launched in the early '90s, there were only two games released alongside it in every major region: *Super Mario World* and *F-Zero*. Using the Super Nintendo's built-in Mode 7 effects, the creators of *F-Zero* found a way to bend and spin background pixels very quickly. The effect was almost 3D and gave the new sci-fi racing title some of the fastest gameplay ever seen.

Other racing series may have fun power-ups and flashy real-world rides, but F-Zero is all about one thing—speed! Ever since the original installment, players have marveled at the series' crazy pace and challenging racetracks. Instead of your average racing vehicles, F-Zero drivers are strapped into ultra-fast hover cars that top out around 1000 miles per hour. With machines moving that fast, players must maneuver safely around the track or face destroying their car—and chances of winning—in a fiery blaze.

F-Zero is set in 2560, a time when intergalactic travel and alien technology make F-Zero races the most exciting sport in the universe. (The prize money is also highly sought after.) Drivers like Captain Falcon, Samurai Goro, Black Shadow, and more must put their hover driving skills to the test. Will you join them?

PLAY IT ON:
Wii U, 3DS, GC, and more

GENRE:
Sports & Fighting

RATING:
E–T

FIRST SEEN:
1990

DID YOU KNOW?

F-Zero X for the Nintendo 64 introduced the racer James McCloud. The character's name and design are a reference to Fox's father in the Star Fox series.

MADE BY:
Nintendo

Played it! ☐   My Rating: ☆☆☆☆☆

My Favorite Moment: _____

Notes: _____

_____

44

MARIO SPORTS

PLAY IT ON:
3DS, Wii U, Wii, and more

GENRE:
Sports & Fighting

RATING:
E

FIRST SEEN:
1995

MADE BY:
Nintendo

Before everyone's favorite plumber began competing in sporting events of his own, Mario could be found as the chair umpire in *Tennis* for the NES, as well as a referee in the original console *Punch-Out!!* game (#42 on our list). But it wasn't until the release of *Mario's Tennis* for the often-forgotten Virtual Boy that Nintendo's mascot got his first real taste of sporting glory.

Though it started with a focus on tennis and golf, the Mario Sports series has expanded to almost every sport on Earth. Over the past 20 years, players have traveled to the Mushroom Kingdom to compete in soccer, baseball, basketball, volleyball, and more. Mario has even teamed up with long-time rival Sonic to go for the gold at the summer and winter Olympic games.

The roster of Mario Sports titles is always brimming with classic Mario friends and enemies, such as Luigi, Yoshi, Princess Peach, and Bowser. *Mario Sports Superstars* for the 3DS is the first title in the franchise to feature four of the series' main sporting events (tennis, golf, baseball, and soccer) all in one game. It even includes horse racing! Whether you're working up a sweat or just horsing around, you're bound to have an exciting time.

DID YOU KNOW?
Pikmin (#75 on our list) can be found in *Mario Golf: Toadstool Tour* for the GameCube. On certain holes, when players hit their ball into patches of flowers, they'll send the tiny creatures flying.

Played it! ☐   My Rating: ☆☆☆☆☆
My Favorite Moment: _____
Notes: _____
_____

WII SPORTS

You know a series is special when your grandma asks if she can play! The Wii Sports games may not have the best graphics or a legendary story, but they have brought new players and a whole lot of movement into the world of gaming. The original title came with the Nintendo Wii, the surprise console hit that revolutionized motion controls. Tennis, golf, baseball, bowling, and boxing were the first sports in the franchise. Each game lets players make simple, realistic movements with the Wii's special motion-controlled Wiimotes. With the right timing, power, and aim, you can bowl a strike, throw a punch, or drive a golf ball to the green.

The sequel to *Wii Sports*, dubbed *Wii Sports Resort*, focused on the Wii's new Motion Plus technology and a beautiful sporting resort called Wuhu Island. With even more precise motion control, players can go head to head in disc golf, sword fighting, basketball, archery, and more.

Over the years, these games have helped players get active, and they've even been used as a form of physical therapy for patients who need to build muscles and improve their range of motion. Old or young, gamer or not, anyone can find something to enjoy in the Wii Sports series, and that makes it truly a home run.

DID YOU KNOW?

The golf courses in the original *Wii Sports* are modeled after the courses in the classic Golf game for NES.

PLAY IT ON:
Wii U and Wii

GENRE:
Sports & Fighting

RATING:
E–E10+

FIRST SEEN:
2006

MADE BY:
Nintendo

Played it! ☐ My Rating: ☆☆☆☆☆
My Favorite Moment: _____
Notes: _____

46

SUPER SMASH BROS.

PLAY IT ON:
Wii, Wii U,
Nintendo 3Ds,
and more

GENRE:
Sports &
Fighting

RATING:
E–T

**FIRST
SEEN:**
1999

MADE BY:
Nintendo

What could be better than a game starring a classic Nintendo character? How about a series that stars *every* classic Nintendo character in the ultimate fighting showdown?

The first *Super Smash Bros.* was released for the Nintendo 64 in 1999 and was an immediate hit with fans. Since the original, Smash Bros. titles have been developed for the GameCube, Wii, Wii U, and 3DS. The Smash Bros. roster has grown from 12 combatants to over 50, and has even

DID YOU KNOW?

If you hold the ZL or ZR button when selecting a Star Fox stage in *Super Smash Bros.* for Wii U, you'll unlock classic Star Fox dialogue. Just make sure you don't have any Star Fox characters in the fight, or it won't work.

featured guest stars from non-Nintendo franchises like Sonic, Pac-Man, and Mega Man.

The Smash Bros. games pit players against each other in an arena with floating platforms. Unlike traditional fighting games, the objective is to knock your opponents so far off the stage that they can't recover. Characters are flung farther off the stage depending on the amount of damage they've taken from a hit. Players win by being the last fighter standing or by having the most knockouts after a time limit. Stage environments, items, and the number of players all factor in when attempting to win a round. The Smash Bros. games are some of the best multiplayer titles ever made, with some games allowing up to eight players at once!

In the game, players learn the Nintendo all-stars are actually toys being manipulated by an all-powerful being known simply as The Master Hand. This giant floating hand is featured as the final boss in many of the series' single-player modes. The Master Hand can use all sorts of tricky attacks and maneuvers, making it one high five you may want to avoid. But don't stay away too long. Seven years after the release of *Super Smash Bros. Melee*, players discovered a special glitch that let them fight as the mighty Master Hand!

WHAT TO PLAY NEXT:
Pokkén Fighters
ARMS
Power Stone

TOP SERIES PICKS:
Super Smash Bros. 64 (N64, 1999)
Super Smash Bros. Melee
(GC, 2001)
Super Smash Bros. for Wii U
(Wii U, 2014)

YOU'LL LIKE THESE GAMES IF...
You want to body slam Pikachu.

Played it! ☐   My Rating: ☆☆☆☆☆
My Favorite Moment: _____
Notes: _____
_____

47

STREET FIGHTER

PLAY IT ON:
PS4, Switch, PC,
and more

GENRE:
Sports &
Fighting

RATING:
E10+–T

**FIRST
SEEN:**
1987

MADE BY:
Capcom

In the world of fighting video games, no series has had more impact than Capcom's arcade hit *Street Fighter*. The original *Street Fighter* wasn't very popular, but still laid much of the groundwork for the series. It was the launch of *Street Fighter II*, four years later, that really shook up the arcade scene and started the fighting game craze of the '90s. While the first *Street Fighter* introduced concepts like six-button controls and special attacks, the sequel improved upon the setup with a combo system, unique characters, and smoother graphics. *Street Fighter II* was a massive success, earning Capcom over two billion dollars in quarters during its arcade lifespan.

The Street Fighter roster consists of different fighters from around the globe, each with their own remarkable fighting techniques and background. There have been dozens of new fighters added over the years, but only two have been playable in every single version: Ryu of Japan and Ken of the United States. Both have gone on to become the mascots of the Street Fighter series, with Ryu usually taking the spotlight as the fan favorite.

Each match consists of players fighting one-on-one against a real-world or computer opponent. To claim victory, a player must drain their opponent's health bar to zero with well-timed attacks and smart defense. Special moves, like Ryu's signature *Hadouken fireball*, can add even more depth to a player's fighting style. Winning two out of three rounds gets a fighter declared the overall winner of the match.

The series has become so popular that professional tournaments are held every year with *Street Fighter* as the main event. The champions are awarded thousands of dollars and global recognition. Do you have the guts and dedication to become one of the best?

DID YOU KNOW?

The combo system in *Street Fighter II* was actually a bug that let players land hits directly after the first attack. It made the game more about skill than luck, and the developers decided to keep it.

WHAT TO PLAY NEXT:
The Marvel vs. Capcom series
The Tekken series
The Injustice series

TOP SERIES PICKS:
Street Fighter II Turbo (SNES, 1993)
*Super Street Fighter II Turbo HD
Remix* (X360, PS3, 2008)
Street Fighter V (PS4, PC, 2014)

YOU'LL LIKE THESE GAMES IF...
You want to become a virtual
martial arts master.

Played it! ☐   My Rating: ☆☆☆☆☆

My Favorite Moment: _____

Notes: _____

_____

48

OLLIOLLI

PLAY IT ON:
PS4, XOne,
PSVita, and more

GENRE:
Sports &
Fighting

RATING:
E–T

**FIRST
SEEN:**
2014

MADE BY:
Roll7

With the introduction of *Tony Hawk's Pro Skater* for PlayStation in the late '90s, the gaming world was set ablaze with the desire to trick every gap, carve every corner, and grind every ledge. Extreme sports, especially skateboarding, were a hot new trend. But eventually, the extreme-sports fad wore out, and even the best of the skating games got a bit stale.

Flash forward to 2014's *OlliOlli* for the PlayStation Vita, a fresh new take on the skating genre. Unlike traditional skateboarding titles with free-roaming 3D levels, *OlliOlli* approached the world of skating with a side-scrolling arcade feel. The pixelated visuals and simple controls made the game easy to learn but difficult to master.

In both *OlliOlli* and *OlliOlli 2*, players must string together as many ridiculous tricks and grinds as they can on their way through different challenging environments. One trip, one fall, or one wrong move, and it's game over. Between both games, there are lots of levels to unlock. While none are too long, the thrill of being one mistake away from failure makes crossing the finish line with a new high score that much more exciting. The OlliOlli series is just tough enough to keep players coming back for more. No helmet required.

DID YOU KNOW?
An *ollie* (spelled without the *e* in the series title) is a basic skateboarding move that's often used to kick off more complex tricks. Skaters perform ollies by pushing down on the back of their boards while jumping.

Played it! ☐ My Rating: ☆☆☆☆☆

My Favorite Moment: _____

Notes: _____

_____

FORZA

While some series let players experience worlds and adventures far beyond their wildest dreams, other games focus on exciting real-world wonders. The Forza universe brings some of these wonders to life in the form of realistic cars and racing. The series features a selection of literally hundreds of vehicles from well-known automotive brands like Lamborghini, Ferrari, and Mercedes-Benz. Not only do the vehicles in the Forza series look like their real-life counterparts, they also handle and perform just like they would if a real person was behind the wheel. The settings for the races are based on authentic locations, such as the Australian Outback, the Colorado Rocky Mountains, and the Indianapolis Motor Speedway. Weather elements and night races have been added over the years to challenge players even more.

The more recent Forza titles have introduced an online auction house, where players use their in-game credits to bid against others or sell unwanted rides. Many vehicles can go for millions of credits in the auction house, and players are always on the lookout for so-called *Unicorn Cars*, or very rare cars. Though rare like unicorns, these cars don't have horns. They make up for their lack of magical abilities by revving gamers' engines.

PLAY IT ON:
XOne, X360, and Xbox

GENRE:
Sports & Fighting

RATING:
E–T

FIRST SEEN:
2005

MADE BY:
Microsoft Studios

DID YOU KNOW?

Forza is an Italian word that means "power, force, or strength."

Played it! ☐   My Rating: ☆☆☆☆☆

My Favorite Moment: _____

Notes: _____

_____

50

FIFA

PLAY IT ON:
PS4, XOne,
Switch, and more

GENRE:
Sports &
Fighting

RATING:
E

**FIRST
SEEN:**
1993

MADE BY:
EA Sports

Because soccer, which is known to most of the world as *football*, is the most popular sport in existence, it comes as no surprise that there have been hundreds of different soccer video games released over the years. Though it's hard to say which individual soccer game is the best of the bunch, the FIFA series is easily the most popular.

The Fédération Internationale de Football Association, or FIFA, has been around for over 100 years. The first FIFA video game was released in 1993, and in the 20+ years since it launched, the FIFA series has sold more than 100 million games and is one of the best-selling sports video games of all time.

The gameplay of the FIFA series has grown from pixelated soccer basics to realistic matches with advanced player-and-ball physics. The classic eleven-on-eleven battle to score the most goals never looked better or felt more authentic. Recent FIFA titles have even given players a special Journey mode that lets them live the life of an up-and-coming soccer star who must prove himself in the world of professional footballers. If you've ever enjoyed kicking around a soccer ball, you should make playing the FIFA series your newest goal.

DID YOU KNOW?

The FIFA World Cup is the most watched sporting event in history. An estimated 3.2 billion viewers tuned in for the 2014 World Cup finale.

Played it! ☐   My Rating: ☆☆☆☆☆

My Favorite Moment: _____

Notes: _____

_____

NBA 2K

The crowd goes wild as you catch a breakaway pass from a teammate and throw down an earth-shattering dunk. With seconds on the clock, you land a 3-pointer that pulls your team ahead. Pro basketball players experience these thrills when they're on the court, and you can join in by playing the NBA 2K series in your own living room.

The NBA 2K series is updated yearly to showcase current teams, new gameplay modes, and more realistic graphics. Players have the option of choosing well-known teams and professionals, or creating their own characters and guiding them through the highs and lows of becoming b-ball superstars. In this mode, known as MyCareer, players can upgrade different stats to improve their characters' skills, and can transform their custom character into the ultimate ball handler, a sharpshooting forward, or any number of other talented team members.

In the MyTeam mode, players manage their own NBA squad, picking everything from their team's jersey design to offensive and defensive plays. NBA 2K offers loads of options and the best basketball action in video games. Will you get benched or become an NBA legend?

PLAY IT ON:
PS4, XOne, Switch, and more

GENRE:
Sports & Fighting

RATING:
E

FIRST SEEN:
1999

MADE BY:
2K Sports

DID YOU KNOW?

Many of the songs featured in the NBA 2K series were hand-picked by popular hip-hop artists like Jay Z, Pharrell Williams, and DJ Khaled.

Played it! ☐ My Rating: ☆☆☆☆☆

My Favorite Moment: _____

Notes: _____

_____

52

ROCKET LEAGUE

Realistic games like basketball, soccer, and hockey are all well and good, but they're way more enjoyable when played with rocket-powered cars wearing silly hats.

Rocket League isn't like any sport you've ever seen or played. Teams of tricked-out vehicles take to the field to flip, smash, and zoom their way to victory. The original mode, a take on soccer, consists of different colored squads attempting to knock an enormous ball into their opponent's goal. Players can use speed boosts to set up a shot, defend their side of the

PLAY IT ON:
PS4, XOne, Switch, and more

GENRE:
Sports & Fighting

RATING:
E

FIRST SEEN:
2015

MADE BY:
Psyonix

DID YOU KNOW?

In February of 2017, *Rocket League* teamed up with Hot Wheels to bring two iconic cars into the game. The classic Twin Mill III and Bone Shaker vehicles can be purchased as downloadable content.

field, or simply wreak havoc on an opponent's car. The *Rocket League* vehicles can also jump, flip, spin, and fly through the air when needed, adding some nice pizzazz to the average shot.

Players can choose different body types, as well as hundreds of other customizable features like paint jobs, tires, antenna ornaments, and more. All together there are 10 billion possibilities. The two most popular ways to personalize a car is with a zany topper or a wild boost stream. Want to dress your dune buggy in a pirate hat and have it shoot money out its backside? Go for it. None of the changes made to a car's appearance affect its abilities while playing. It's just fun to add some personal flair to your flashy new ride.

Rocket League creators Psyonix are constantly releasing new cars, toppers, and modes via digital updates to the game. Hockey and basketball modes have been added to the mix, as well as a Rumble mode that puts a twist on the classic soccer game by introducing power-ups. *Rocket League* is one of the best online and local multiplayer games in recent years, with millions of players worldwide. Just be careful. Once you pick it up, you'll want to press your pedal to the metal all day, every day.

WHAT TO PLAY NEXT:
Mario Strikers Charged
Videoball
Towerfall

TOP DOWNLOADABLE UPGRADES:
Revenge of the Battle Cars
Back to the Future
Batman v Superman

YOU'LL LIKE THESE GAMES IF...
You're tired of normal sports.

Played it! ☐   My Rating: ☆☆☆☆☆

My Favorite Moment: _____

Notes: _____

_____

53

MARVEL VS. CAPCOM

PLAY IT ON:
PS4, XOne, PC,
and more

GENRE:
Sports &
Fighting

RATING:
T

**FIRST
SEEN:**
1996

MADE BY:
Capcom

Superheroes and video games are a match made in heaven. Comic-book fans and gamers the world over have been battling as their favorite fictional heroes for decades, but it wasn't until the release of *X-Men vs. Street Fighter* in 1996 that both sides realized the pure awesomeness of a crossover fighting game. This was the beginning of an epic throw down between Marvel, the king of comics, and the legendary game developer Capcom.

DID YOU KNOW?

Although the series is known for unusual characters, *Ultimate Marvel vs. Capcom 3*'s Phoenix Wright takes the cake. Phoenix comes from his own series where he stars as a bumbling lawyer. His moves include tossing paperwork, digging up evidence, and sneezing on unsuspecting opponents.

The *Marvel vs. Capcom* series is easily the greatest superhero and gaming crossover title to ever grace an arcade or TV screen. The franchise is chock-full of classic heroes and villains; in the Marvel corner, we have Wolverine, Spider-Man, Captain America, and many more. Capcom leads the way with dozens of popular fighters, including a few that can be found in this very book, such as Ryu (Street Fighter), Zero (Mega Man X), and Amaterasu (Ōkami). Fighters have custom attacks and finishing moves that stem from their history in the world of comics or gaming—and sometimes both.

Players assemble teams of two or three combatants from the series' monstrous roster and go head-to-head with teams controlled by the computer or a friend. By chaining together combos and switching characters at the right times, players can lower the enemy squad's life energy and knock out their members one by one. The team that manages to stay alive in a best-of-three match is crowned the winner. Players will want to try different combinations of fighters to see which team works best with their personal style. You have to think on your feet in Marvel vs. Capcom, as it's one of the fastest, most chaotic fighting series ever made.

If you're not too busy geeking out over all the awesome characters and moves, you should try your hand at some online matches in the most recent game, *Marvel vs. Capcom: Infinite*. Just don't Hulk out and throw your controller through the wall when you lose a match or two!

WHAT TO PLAY NEXT:
The Street Fighter series
The Injustice series
The Smash Bros. series

TOP SERIES PICKS:
Marvel vs. Capcom 2 (DC, 2000)
Ultimate Marvel vs. Capcom 3
(PS3, X360, 2011)
Marvel vs. Capcom: Infinite
(PS4, XOne, PC, 2017)

YOU'LL LIKE THESE GAMES IF...
You wish you were one of
the Avengers.

Played it! ☐ My Rating: ☆☆☆☆☆
My Favorite Moment: _____
Notes: _____
_____

54

SSX

PLAY IT ON:
PS3, Xbox 360, Wii, and more

GENRE:
Sports & Fighting

RATING:
E–E10+

FIRST SEEN:
2000

MADE BY:
EA Sports BIG

The world of extreme sports is already pretty, well, extreme. Professional athletes push the limits of gravity and pull off tricks that seem impossible. It's only in the world of gaming that these amazing feats can be topped.

The Snowboarding Supercross series, known simply as SSX, has been treating players to insane snowboarding tricks and courses since the start of the millennium. Though the original SSX for PlayStation 2 introduced the game's trademark speed and funky fresh attitude, it was the sequel that really pumped up the in-air maneuvers. This game, dubbed *SSX Tricky*, gave players the chance to pull off *Uber Tricks*, snowboarding moves so ridiculous and dangerous that no real-world athlete could come close to landing them. Riders can incorporate crazy breakdance moves, spin their board like a propeller, and even ride it like a pony, all while hanging in midair.

Every SSX game to date has focused on two main types of snowboarding challenges. The first is a classic race down the mountain, with players searching for shortcuts and using tricks to gain speed boosts. The second is known simply as "Show-off" and involves racking up as many points as possible by landing Uber Tricks and other extraordinary combos. Face it, there's "snow" series trickier than SSX.

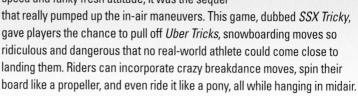

DID YOU KNOW?

SSX on Tour for the GameCube features some unlikely special characters: Mario, Luigi, and Princess Peach! They're a bit out of place among the game's realistic snowboarders, but these Mushroom Kingdom celebrities sure know how to hit the slopes.

Played it! ☐   My Rating: ☆☆☆☆☆

My Favorite Moment: _____

Notes: _____

HOT SHOTS GOLF

Not every sports game has to include rocket-powered cars or over-the-top athletic action. Sometimes it's nice to just relax and sink a few easy putts. Golf has long been a game of precision and power, and it's played by millions of folks around the world. The Hot Shots Golf series, known as Everyone's Golf in Europe and Japan, is one of gaming's best takes on this easygoing sport.

The PlayStation exclusive is known for its mix of cartoonish designs and realistic golf physics. The golfers featured throughout the series each have their own distinct look and personality, as well as hilarious animations that can be seen when they win big or fail hard. The golf gameplay in Hot Shots, much like real life, is all about setup. Players can switch out clubs to change where and how their ball is hit. Once a shot is lined up, players must time their swing to put just the right amount of power behind the ball. Normal golf hazards like bodies of water, sand, and trees stand between your golfer and the sunny green.

You don't have to be a huge fan of golf to find *Hot Shots Golf* enjoyable. Just remember: In golf, it's the lowest number of hits that wins, so this is one video game where you *don't* want to shoot for the high score.

PLAY IT ON:
PSVita, PS3, PS2
and more

GENRE:
Sports &
Fighting

RATING:
E–E 10+

**FIRST
SEEN:**
1997

DID YOU KNOW?

Sony superstar duo Ratchet and Clank, as well as Jak and Daxter, make guest appearances in PS2's *Hot Shots Golf Fore!* Ratchet and Jak are both playable golfers, with Clank and Daxter acting as caddies.

MADE BY:
Camelot/Sony
Computer
Entertainment

Played it! ☐ My Rating: ☆☆☆☆☆
My Favorite Moment: _____
Notes: _____

56

MADDEN NFL

PLAY IT ON:
PS4, XOne, X360,
and more

GENRE:
Sports &
Fighting

RATING:
E

**FIRST
SEEN:**
1988

MADE BY:
EA Sports

You look over the heads of your linemen to see eleven enormous opponents, all with the sole goal of stopping you from moving forward. You scan the field and bark out audibles to help your team adjust their offense. Hut! Hut! Hike! The ball is snapped, and after a scuffle, you find your running back flying across the end zone. The ball is up. It's caught. Touchdown!

The excitement and drama of football, known as *American football* throughout most of the world, is a big part of many sports fans' lives. The

DID YOU KNOW?

Professional football players featured on the cover of a Madden NFL game are said to fall under the dreaded "Madden Curse." The superstition comes from the surprising number of top athletes who are chosen for the Madden cover that go on to suffer injuries or have terrible seasons following the game's release.

Madden NFL series has been letting regular folks experience this rush firsthand, for over 25 years, putting players in the cleats of the National Football League's best and brightest. What started as a pixelated romp in the early days of home-console gaming has grown into one of the most popular and realistic digital franchises to date.

The core gameplay of the Madden series is based on the standard rules and regulations of NFL football. Colorful game commentary, real-world locations, and hundreds of classic football plays and formations make many of the gridiron match-ups seem like the real deal. Those who want a faster or more challenging experience can tweak the game settings to their liking with customized quarter lengths and computer difficulty levels. If you're not up for tackling computer players you can always go head to head with a friend, both locally or online.

The Madden series launches a new football title every fall, with an updated roster and a host of new features for players to dive into. Aside from simply playing through a regular season of matchups, football fans can also try out Franchise mode, which lets players make all the big decisions for any professional football team, like which players will start, what kind of drills to run in practice, and how to handle devastating injuries. The breathtaking world of the NFL is at your fingertips. Don't fumble this opportunity.

WHAT TO PLAY NEXT:
The Tecmo Bowl series
The NFL Street series
The FIFA series

TOP SERIES PICKS:
Madden '95 (GEN, SNES, 1994)
Madden 2005
(PS2, Xbox, GC, 2004)
Madden 18 (PS4, XOne, 2017)

YOU'LL LIKE THESE GAMES IF...
You dream of being the star quarterback.

Played it! ☐   My Rating: ☆☆☆☆☆

My Favorite Moment: _____

Notes: _____

_____

57

EXCITEBIKE

PLAY IT ON:
3DS, Wii U, Wii,
and more

GENRE:
Sports &
Fighting

RATING:
E

**FIRST
SEEN:**
1984

MADE BY:
Nintendo

Starting its life on the NES, *Excitebike* is a Nintendo classic through and through. Players attempt to position their Excitebike rider on one of four racing paths while also controlling the speed of their motorbikes. If a bike accelerates too quickly or for too long, it will overheat and be forced to cool down, costing players valuable time and distance. While avoiding track hazards, like mud and other riders, players must try to land epic jumps, hit boost strips, and keep their balance as they strive to set a new course record.

Despite its name, the Excitebike series isn't just about racing bikes. *Excite Truck* was a launch title for the Wii in 2006, featuring souped-up trucks with insane speed and monster jumps. The follow up was *ExciteBots: Trick Racing*, also for the Wii, which focused on bizarre animal machines that could actually run on robotic legs before transforming into vehicles. The game lets players perform silly stunts, such as collecting ingredients for a giant sandwich or throwing darts at a huge dartboard mid-race.

Whether it's bikes, trucks, or frog robots, racing fans will find something to knock their socks off in the Excitebike series. Now doesn't that sound excite-ing?

DID YOU KNOW?

The Switch title *Mario Kart 8 Deluxe* features a racetrack called *Excitebike Arena*, which is modeled after classic ramps and obstacles from the original game!

Played it! ☐   My Rating: ☆☆☆☆☆
My Favorite Moment: _____
Notes: _____
_____

GRAN TURISMO

The first Gran Turismo title for the PlayStation was a labor of love. It took the small team at Polyphony Digital over five years to complete the game, which was one of the first super realistic racing games to feature cars from around the world. With over 10 million copies sold, *Gran Turismo* is the best-selling original PlayStation game of all time.

Though many racing fans like to compare *Gran Turismo* to the Forza series (#49 on our list), the PlayStation-exclusive franchise has been around for nearly a decade longer than Microsoft's racing simulator. Paving the way for titles like Forza, the first Gran Turismo games gave players access to hundreds of lifelike cars and locations, and nearly perfected the feeling of burning rubber.

The most recent game in the series, *Gran Turismo Sport*, is the start of a whole new racing era. The game showcases exclusive online racing tournaments where players can represent their country or their favorite brand of automobile. A virtual-reality showcase, called *VR Tour Mode*, is also available with the help of the PlayStation VR headset. With an ever-growing lineup of cars and racing events, it's safe to say the Gran Turismo series won't be slowing down anytime soon.

DID YOU KNOW?

Gran Turismo 6 for the PlayStation 3 has more than 1,000 real-world cars to choose from. You're going to need a bigger garage.

PLAY IT ON:
PS4, PS3, PS2, and more

GENRE:
Sports & Fighting

RATING:
E–T

FIRST SEEN:
1997

MADE BY:
Polyphony Digital

Played it! ☐   My Rating: ☆☆☆☆☆
My Favorite Moment: _____
Notes: _____
_____

59

EARTHBOUND

PLAY IT ON:
Wii U, 3DS,
SNES, and more

GENRE:
Role Playing &
Strategy

RATING:
E–T

**FIRST
SEEN:**
1989

MADE BY:
Nintendo

EarthBound stinks. At least that's what the ads for the 1995 Super Nintendo game would have you believe. When the cult classic role-playing title launched for Nintendo's 16-bit system, it came bundled with a strategy guide full of scratch-and-sniff stickers. With the tagline "This game stinks!" it's no wonder *EarthBound* didn't sell as well as its Japanese counterpart, known as *Mother 2*.

EarthBound is actually a sequel to the Japanese game *Mother*, a quirky RPG produced for the Nintendo Famicom. When it came time to bring Mother to other regions of the world, Nintendo found it would be too expensive and focused their efforts on the upcoming Super NES instead. *Mother* was finally released worldwide as *EarthBound Beginnings* for the Wii U a staggering 26 years after its Japanese launch.

EarthBound is centered on a young lad named Ness who hails from the town of Onett. When a mysterious meteorite crashes near his house, Ness discovers Buzz Buzz, a powerful insect sent from the future. Buzz Buzz warns our hero that the wicked alien Giygas will plunge the world into darkness if Ness does not collect eight special melodies and attempt to destroy him. With this warning, Ness grabs his trusty baseball bat and heads out into the great unknown. As the game progresses, Ness discovers psychic powers and teams up with new friends to eradicate Giygas.

Though *EarthBound* is a traditional role-playing game, its plot, settings, characters, and combat are quite unique and silly. When battling enemies, none of the game's heroes can be seen on screen. Instead, they're represented by rolling meters that display health and psychic powers. The baddies in the game may be the most bizarre part, with opponents such as Annoying Old Party Man, Smelly Ghost, and Big Pile of Puke standing in your way. The more you play the EarthBound series, the weirder everything gets—and that's the best part.

DID YOU KNOW?

A follow-up to *EarthBound* was planned, but eventually scrapped, for Nintendo 64. Some story elements and characters ended up in the Japan-only game *Mother 3* for the Game Boy Advance. Although it's technically a sequel, the game doesn't star Ness or any of his *EarthBound* allies.

WHAT TO PLAY NEXT:
Chrono Trigger
Undertale
The Mario & Luigi series

TOP SERIES PICKS:
EarthBound Beginnings
(Wii U, 2015)
EarthBound (SNES, 1995)
Mother 3 (Japan Only)
(GBA, 2006)

YOU'LL LIKE THESE GAMES IF...
You're kind of a weirdo.

Played it! ☐ My Rating: ☆☆☆☆☆
My Favorite Moment: _____
Notes: _____
_____

60

FINAL FANTASY

PLAY IT ON:
PS4, XOne,
SNES, and more

GENRE:
Role Playing &
Strategy

RATING:
E-T

**FIRST
SEEN:**
1987

MADE BY:
Square Enix

The word *final* is usually used to describe events that are coming to an end—the final fight, the NBA finals, the final countdown. You get the idea. When creator Hironobu Sakaguchi was coming up with the name for his new role-playing game, he decided on *Final Fantasy* for two reasons: If the game wasn't a success, he was going to quit the gaming industry and go back to school, and Square, the company he worked for, was about to go bankrupt. (Spoiler alert: The game wasn't so final after all.)

Thirty years after the launch of the first Final Fantasy game, the series is still going strong. It has become one of the best-selling gaming franchises of all time and an important part of RPG history. While they have quite a bit in common, every one of the fifteen Final Fantasy games in the main series features a brand-new story and cast of characters. When it comes to combat and gameplay, players can choose a Final Fantasy title at random and not have to worry about learning the background of the series.

The settings mix science fiction and fantasy, creating magical environments that also have a futuristic feel. While progressing through the games, players are often thrown into battles against mighty creatures and supernatural beings. As more battles are won, characters level up, gaining more hit points (HP), new attacks, and powerful magical abilities.

The world of Final Fantasy has evolved from pixels and 8-bit blips into one of the most stunning and melodious RPG adventures on the planet. Here's to another 30 years of Final Fantasy!

DID YOU KNOW?

When North American RPG fans picked up *Final Fantasy II* and *III* for the Super Nintendo, they were actually playing *Final Fantasy IV* and *VI*. That's because many of the early games in the series were only released in Japan, forcing some of the titles to be renumbered elsewhere in the world.

WHAT TO PLAY NEXT:
The Dragon Quest series
The Bravely Default series
The Xenoblade Chronicles series

TOP SERIES PICKS:
Final Fantasy VII (PS, 1997)
Final Fantasy X (PS2, 2001)
Final Fantasy XV (PS4, XOne, 2016)

YOU'LL LIKE THESE GAMES IF...
You live for magic battles.

Played it! ☐   My Rating: ☆☆☆☆☆
My Favorite Moment: _____
Notes: _____
_____

61

CHRONO TRIGGER

PLAY IT ON:
DS, PS3, Wii,
and more

GENRE:
Role Playing &
Strategy

RATING:
E–T

**FIRST
SEEN:**
1995

MADE BY:
Square Enix

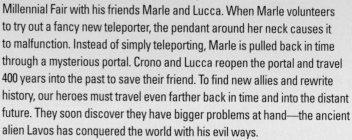

What do you get when you combine the talented developer behind the Final Fantasy series with the world-famous artist responsible for the *Dragon Ball* line of comics and cartoons? The answer is *Chrono Trigger*, a Super Nintendo RPG brimming with charming characters and a far-out timeline.

The adventure begins with the silent protagonist Crono on his way to the nearby Millennial Fair with his friends Marle and Lucca. When Marle volunteers to try out a fancy new teleporter, the pendant around her neck causes it to malfunction. Instead of simply teleporting, Marle is pulled back in time through a mysterious portal. Crono and Lucca reopen the portal and travel 400 years into the past to save their friend. To find new allies and rewrite history, our heroes must travel even farther back in time and into the distant future. They soon discover they have bigger problems at hand—the ancient alien Lavos has conquered the world with his evil ways.

Chrono Trigger's battle system isn't quite as complicated as your average retro RPG, so it's a great game for beginners and veterans alike. The original *Chrono Trigger* journey has been rereleased on the PlayStation and Nintendo DS, while a true sequel dubbed *Chrono Cross* launched in 1999. It's certainly a series that's worth your time.

DID YOU KNOW?

Chrono Trigger has more than ten different endings that can be unlocked by attempting, winning, or losing certain battles. In one ending, called "The Dream Project," Crono and pals get to meet pixelated versions of the game's creators.

Played it! ☐ My Rating: ☆☆☆☆☆
My Favorite Moment: _____
Notes: _____
_____

MARIO & LUIGI

Mamma mia! Classic adventures, go-kart races, sports, and parties just weren't enough for the Mushroom Kingdom's famous plumber duo, so they decided to conquer the world of RPGs. While *Super Mario RPG* and *Paper Mario* both launched first, the Mario & Luigi series stands out with its hilarious writing and tag-team combat system.

Superstar Saga, the first game in the series, is the perfect example of the silly story lines. When villains steal Princess Peach's elegant voice and replace it with explosives, it's up to Mario and Luigi to help their friend. Over the years, the mustachioed brothers have also traveled through time, been swallowed by Bowser, and even teamed up with Paper Mario.

The series focuses on basic individual attacks and special team maneuvers that cause serious damage. Mario classics like wooden hammers and fire flowers can be used during battle, and the brothers work together to perform powerful moves. Timing is also a big factor in battle— a perfectly timed press of a button can lead to a stronger attack or a greater defense. Teamwork is the key to winning, especially for these brothers.

PLAY IT ON:
3DS, Wii U, DS, and more

GENRE:
Role Playing & Strategy

RATING:
E–E10+

FIRST SEEN:
2003

DID YOU KNOW?

To promote the release (and humor) of *Mario & Luigi: Superstar Saga*, Nintendo held a knock-knock joke contest. Over 1,300 jokes were submitted, but only the best were chosen as winners.

MADE BY:
Nintendo

Played it! ☐   My Rating: ☆☆☆☆☆
My Favorite Moment: _____
Notes: _____
_____

63

FIRE EMBLEM

PLAY IT ON:
3DS, Wii U, DS,
and more

GENRE:
Role Playing &
Strategy

RATING:
E–T

**FIRST
SEEN:**
1990

MADE BY:
Nintendo

Losing a life usually isn't a big deal when it comes to video games. Sure, you might drop some loot or have to start from a distant save point, but most games bring your character back over and over until you've accomplished your current goal. The Fire Emblem series is infamous for not following this time-honored gaming tradition.

DID YOU KNOW?

Marth and Roy were unlockable fighters in *Super Smash Bros. Melee* for the GameCube. Two years before Fire Emblem launched outside of Japan, their appearance made many English-speaking players wonder who these characters were and how they made it onto the roster.

The heroes of Fire Emblem are plagued by something called *permadeath*, meaning if they die in battle, they're lost forever from your band of heroes. The high stakes make every move in the Fire Emblem games so important. While newer Fire Emblem adventures feature casual modes, where fallen heroes can return, many Fire Emblem fans prefer playing with the classic permadeath limitations. It is the only way to truly experience the intensity and strategy the series is known for.

Although there are many different Fire Emblem story lines, the series features the same basic battle system. Unlike classic RPGs where players can randomly encounter an enemy or sneak up and deliver the first blow, Fire Emblem gives both sides opportunities to move and attack across a gridded battlefield map. Players can charge the enemy straight on by bringing their combatant within fighting range, or they can retreat to a far-off spot to heal. Depending on weapon range and magic abilities, many heroes can attack from a distance or help protect their nearby friends.

Like many RPG titles, the Fire Emblem games have characters that can be enhanced with new armor, weapons, and unique skills as they level up. Recent Fire Emblem titles let players customize the main heroes in many ways, even letting them marry other characters within the game! But don't get too attached to your Fire Emblem friends if you're playing with permadeath. One wrong move could mean you'll never see them again.

WHAT TO PLAY NEXT:
Final Fantasy Tactics
The Advance War series
Tokyo Mirage Sessions #FE

TOP SERIES PICKS:
Fire Emblem (GBA, 2003)
Fire Emblem Awakening
(3DS, 2012)
Fire Emblem Fates (3DS, 2016)

YOU'LL LIKE THESE GAMES IF...
You always have a battle plan.

Played it! ☐ My Rating: ☆☆☆☆☆☆

My Favorite Moment: _____

Notes: _____

_____

UNDERTALE

PLAY IT ON:
PC, PS4, NS, and PS Vita

GENRE:
Role Playing & Strategy

RATING:
E10+ or T

FIRST SEEN:
2015

MADE BY:
Toby Fox

Have you ever felt like giving your enemy a hug or encouraging them to follow their dreams? It may seem like a silly option for an RPG, but it's choices like these that really bring *Undertale's* goofy and meaningful charm to life. Unlike the average RPG, players can take a non-violent approach to each fight, choosing to spare their enemy or even befriend them (though fighting is also an option).

Undertale was made almost entirely by one person; creator Toby Fox worked for nearly three years to complete the game, and even composed all the music. Fox set out to make a game that focused on a player's choices and avoided unnecessary backtracking and grinding. (The term grinding refers to players having to fight the same low-level enemies over and over to become strong enough to move the story forward.)

The plot of *Undertale* follows a small child who falls underground into the world of monsters. The monsters used to live on the surface with the humans, but were sealed away by a magical barrier after a great war. The child must go on a quest to find a way back to the surface.

When the child encounters wacky monsters, like skeleton brothers Papyrus and Sans, players are given the options to fight, spare the opponent, run, use an item, or communicate with the opponent in a positive way. To attack an opponent, players stop a bar on a power meter. To defend from an attack, players move a small heart icon around the screen to avoid little white shapes. The choices of actions in battle are very important and can change the overall outcome of *Undertale's* grand underground adventure. What will you choose to do?

DID YOU KNOW?
Undertale characters Papyrus and Sans are named after different typefaces, or fonts. When both characters speak, their text is shown in their signature typeface.

WHAT TO PLAY NEXT:
EarthBound
The Mario & Luigi series
Cave Story

TOP DOGS TO PET IN BATTLE:
Doggo
Lesser Dog
Dogamy and Dogaressa

YOU'LL LIKE THESE GAMES IF...
You want to befriend your enemies.

Played it! ☐   My Rating: ☆☆☆☆☆

My Favorite Moment: _____

Notes: _____

_____

65

YO-KAI WATCH

PLAY IT ON:
3DS

GENRE:
Role Playing &
Strategy

RATING:
E 10+

**FIRST
SEEN:**
2013

MADE BY:
Level-5

If you've ever had a runny nose or been late for the bus, you may have been visited by a mischievous Yo-kai. In Japanese folklore, Yo-kai are supernatural monsters and spirits that enjoy playing tricks on unsuspecting humans.

In the Yo-kai Watch series, players assume the role of either Nate or Katie, both of whom have the ability to see pesky Yo-kai thanks to the powers of the Yo-kai watch. Once found, a Yo-kai can be battled or bribed with treats, both of which may convince them to join the player's squad. Some Yo-kai are more wicked than others, haunting unknowing victims and causing major problems around the town. You'll need some stellar Yo-kai on your team if you want to defeat them all.

Somewhat similar to the Pokémon series, the battles in the Yo-kai Watch series revolve around a team of six monsters who must use their powers to defeat opponents. Unlike Pokémon, Yo-kai Watch doesn't give players endless time to think through their options. Enemies are constantly attacking, and players must rotate Yo-kai in and out of battle as they choose the best time to strike.

The next time something seems amiss, be on the lookout for the ghostly trail of a Yo-kai. Who knows, you might just find a new friend.

DID YOU KNOW?

In the cartoon, a shark Yo-kai named Steve Jaws is shown talking about new Yo-kai technology being made by his company, Yopple, a reference to Steve Jobs, the legendary co-founder of tech giant Apple.

Played it! ☐   My Rating: ☆☆☆☆☆
My Favorite Moment: _____
Notes: _____
_____

PAPER MARIO

Near the end of the Super Nintendo's life span, Nintendo teamed with Square—the developer known for the Final Fantasy series and *Chrono Trigger*—to create *Super Mario RPG*. The game would go on to become a SNES classic and sell millions of copies. While Square began to work more closely with PlayStation, Nintendo focused on creating *Super Mario RPG 2* for their new Nintendo 64 console.

After playing with different art styles, the developers at Intelligent Systems settled on one that made the characters appear as paper thin cartoons while the world around them kept a standard 3D look. Since it now resembled a pop-up book, the game's name was changed to *Paper Mario* (and *Mario Story* in Japan).

The first two Paper Mario games are based around classic RPG battle systems, and much like the Mario & Luigi games, they use Mario's signature moves and feature classic items for attack and healing. The series is known for its creative take on a paper world, something the last two entries for 3DS and Wii U did best. Players can blow enemies away with a giant fan or use their finger to cut out useful parts of the background. With hilarious characters and an arsenal of Mushroom Kingdom power-ups, the Paper Mario adventures truly unfold before your eyes.

DID YOU KNOW?

Super Paper Mario for the Wii is the only Paper Mario game that doesn't rely on role-playing elements. Instead, the game focuses on classic Mario platforming and the ability to switch from 2D to 3D.

PLAY IT ON:
Wii U, 3DS, GC and more

GENRE:
Role Playing & Strategy

RATING:
E

FIRST SEEN:
2000

MADE BY:
Nintendo

Played it! ☐   My Rating: ☆☆☆☆☆
My Favorite Moment: _____
Notes: _____
_____

67

HARVEST MOON

PLAY IT ON:
3DS, Wii U, PS3,
and more

GENRE:
Role Playing &
Strategy

RATING:
E-E10+

**FIRST
SEEN:**
1996

MADE BY:
Marvelous
Interactive

Video games have a funny way of making even the most boring chore into an entertaining activity. Most folks would groan at the thought of getting up early to feed chickens or harvest vegetables from a massive garden. Yet the Harvest Moon series has found a way to make farming simulation both charming and addictive.

DID YOU KNOW?

Harvest Moon creator Yasuhiro Wada came up with the idea for the farming series when he moved from the laid back country to the bustling streets of Tokyo. He wanted to recreate his childhood experience of living in a peaceful rural area.

In most Harvest Moon titles, characters start out with a small farm and a few barnyard animals. By planting and harvesting crops, as well as collecting milk and eggs from their livestock, they can earn cash to purchase a horse, upgrade tools, buy some tasty treats, and more. The gameplay is based around an internal clock that shows the in-game time of day, as well as the date. Certain happenings take place daily, while bigger events fall on certain days of the week or during certain seasons. Hidden supernatural helpers, such as fairies, can be found hiding in secret caves and will fix broken tools or improve a batch of crops.

Outside of the farm, a nearby town has all sorts of interesting side stories to discover. Town festivals, which happen every few weeks, allow characters to meet and interact with townsfolk in new ways. Some of the Harvest Moon games even let characters get married and have children after they establish their farm.

Due to a weird twist of events, the Harvest Moon series name had to be changed to "Story of Seasons" before the 2015 release of the next title in the franchise. Under any name, these fantastic farming games are worth trying, even if you think it might not be your cup of tea. You may just find yourself plowing, harvesting, and collecting eggs until the cows come home.

WHAT TO PLAY NEXT:
The Animal Crossing series
The Rune Factory series
Stardew Valley

TOP SERIES PICKS:
Harvest Moon (SNES, 1996)
Harvest Moon: Friends of Mineral Town (GBA, 2003)
Story of Seasons (3DS, 2015)

YOU'LL LIKE THESE GAMES IF...
You don't mind getting your hands dirty.

Played it! ☐   My Rating: ☆☆☆☆☆
My Favorite Moment: _____
Notes: _____
_____

68

POKÉMON

PLAY IT ON:
3DS, DS, GBA,
and more

GENRE:
Role Playing &
Strategy

RATING:
E

**FIRST
SEEN:**
1996

MADE BY:
Nintendo

Pokémon creator Satoshi Tajiri spent much of his childhood collecting bugs and tadpoles around his neighborhood in Tokyo. The joy of tracking and capturing these creatures in nature inspired him to come up with the now-famous, monster-catching-and-battling series.

The series follows a main character who has set out on a journey to become the best Pokémon trainer in the region. Trainers must catch and

DID YOU KNOW?

In the original two titles (*Red* and *Blue*), trainers can run into the glitchy Pokémon known as MissingNo by following a list of seemingly random actions. Battling this strange monster multiplies items, but it can also corrupt some of the game's data.

train wild monsters they encounter, leveling them up and teaching them new attacks. By defeating gym leaders and other important figures, trainers can move on to new towns, cities, and routes. Though the settings change with each new main-series entry, the basic concepts are always the same: capture, trade, and battle.

The first Pokémon titles, *Red* and *Blue* (*Red* and *Green* in Japan), feature 151 Pokémon to collect and 8 badges for players to earn in battle. Since these initial games were released, the number of Pokémon has skyrocketed to over 800! New types of Pokémon, not to mention moves, items, rivals, and more, have been introduced over the years. *Pokémon Sun* and *Moon*, released in fall of 2016, are the first games to not have gym badges to collect. Instead, players must complete island trials that reward them with coveted Z crystals.

Despite their popularity, main-series Pokémon titles haven't been featured on a Nintendo home console—yet. The creators of Pokémon are hard at work on an official Pokémon adventure for the hybrid home and portable console, the Nintendo Switch. We have seen Pokémon spin-offs, such as photography game *Pokémon Snap* and fighting game *Pokkén Fighters*, on home consoles, but this will be the first entry in the main series playable on the big screen. If you're a true fan, it doesn't matter what platform the game is on. You've got to play 'em all!

WHAT TO PLAY NEXT:
The Yo-kai Watch series
The Pokémon
Mystery Dungeon series
Ni no Kuni: Wrath of the
White Witch series

TOP SERIES PICKS:
Pokémon Red and *Blue* (GB, 1998)
Pokémon Black and *White*
(DS, 2011)
Pokémon Sun and *Moon*
(3DS, 2016)

YOU'LL LIKE THESE GAMES IF...
You always wanted a pet monster.

Played it! ☐   My Rating: ☆☆☆☆☆
My Favorite Moment: _____
Notes: _____
_____

69

COSTUME QUEST

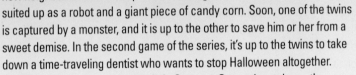

PLAY IT ON:
PC, PS4, XOne,
and more

GENRE:
Role Playing &
Strategy

RATING:
E10+

**FIRST
SEEN:**
2010

MADE BY:
Double Fine

Candy! Not only is it a delicious treat that rots your teeth, it's also at the center of this Halloween-themed, sugar-coated adventure that is brimming with menacing masks and canyon-sized cavities. The Costume Quest series captures the magic and mystery of the Halloween season through the perspective of a heroic group of youngsters.

Choose to play as one of two characters— twins Reynold and Wren, who explore their new neighborhood on a crisp Halloween night, suited up as a robot and a giant piece of candy corn. Soon, one of the twins is captured by a monster, and it is up to the other to save him or her from a sweet demise. In the second game of the series, it's up to the twins to take down a time-traveling dentist who wants to stop Halloween altogether.

When characters enter a battle in Costume Quest, they take on the realistic form of whatever costume they are wearing. With tons of costumes to collect along the way, characters can transform into dinosaurs, wizards, and… french fries? Sure, why not.

Anyone who has ever gone door to door in hopes of a trick or a treat will find the Costume Quest series to be one of the silliest and spookiest role-playing titles they've ever gotten their sugary hands on.

DID YOU KNOW?

Frederator, the studio behind animated hits like *Adventure Time* and *The Fairly OddParents*, is set to produce a *Costume Quest* cartoon series for Amazon streaming services. The show will premiere in 2018.

Played it! ☐ My Rating: ☆☆☆☆☆
My Favorite Moment: _____
Notes: _____

CIVILIZATION

Wouldn't it be great if you could rule the world? In the Civilization games, you can do just that, with some hard work and brilliant planning. Created by legendary game designer Sid Meier, the critically acclaimed Civilization series is known for its deep strategy and reference to real-world history.

Players begin on a virtual game board that is sectioned off into tiles. By building cities, harvesting nearby resources, and waging war on surrounding territories, players can expand their empire and improve their economy. As the game is turn-based, players have plenty of time to think about the next best move for their thriving civilization. The more power and land a player controls, the more they must strategize and plan. Whether you want to develop your people's technology or beef up your army of soldiers, there is always something important to do and somewhere new to conquer.

Each civilization is formed under one of history's greatest leaders, such as George Washington, Mahatma Gandhi, Napoléon Bonaparte, or Augustus Caesar. Though each player's conquest may vary, these game characters are modeled after many of the ideals held by their real-life counterparts. You might just learn something!

PLAY IT ON:
PC, PS, SNES, and more

GENRE:
Role Playing & Strategy

RATING:
E–E10+

FIRST SEEN:
1991

DID YOU KNOW?

CivilizationEDU, a special version of *Civilization* for classrooms, launched in fall of 2017. It uses classic gameplay elements to help students learn more about economics, politics, and critical thinking.

MADE BY:
Firaxis Games

Played it! ☐ My Rating: ☆☆☆☆☆

My Favorite Moment: _____

Notes: _____

_____

71

ANIMAL CROSSING

PLAY IT ON:
3DS, DS, Wii,
and more

GENRE:
Role Playing &
Strategy

RATING:
E

**FIRST
SEEN:**
2001

MADE BY:
Nintendo

Moving to a new place can be scary. There are important items to buy, neighbors to meet, environments to explore, and local shops to discover. The Animal Crossing series takes this uncertainty and gives it an adorable and relaxing spin.

The first *Animal Crossing* game, originally launched in Japan for the Nintendo 64 under the title *Animal Forest*, was introduced to the English-speaking world on the Nintendo GameCube. Players are dropped into a randomly generated town with a handful of animal neighbors, where they can purchase a small house from local business guru Tom Nook. Tom is a Japanese raccoon dog called a tanuki and runs a local shop with clothes, tools, and furniture. As players explore their new home and chat with animal pals, they learn where to find important landmarks such as bridges, waterfalls, and the town square. By selling local fruit, fish, and bugs, players can earn sacks of money, known in the Animal Crossing world as bells. With bells, players can upgrade their houses, buy swanky new furniture, improve their town, and much more.

Personal design is a big part of what makes the Animal Crossing series so enjoyable. Players can customize their house with unique furniture sets and decorate their yard with beautiful plants. The Able Sisters tailor shop sells different outfits and hats, and players can even design their own clothing patterns by hand. Players can even alter other aspects of the game, such as their town flag and town song.

Though the gameplay is very laid back, no two days in an Animal Crossing game are ever the same. You can visit the local museum, greet a new furry resident, enter a fishing contest, or just relax on the beach with some friends. Life is what you make of it.

DID YOU KNOW?

If a player restarts or resets an Animal Crossing game without saving, they will be greeted by the long winded Mr. Resetti, a ranting mole that will go on and on about the dangers of not saving. So always save your game!

WHAT TO PLAY NEXT:
The Harvest Moon series
Tomodachi Life
Fantasy Life

TOP SERIES PICKS:
Animal Crossing (GC, 2001)
Animal Crossing: Wild World
(DS, 2005)
Animal Crossing: New Leaf
(3DS, 2012)

YOU'LL LIKE THESE GAMES IF...
You want to stop and
smell the roses.

Played it! ☐   My Rating: ☆☆☆☆☆
My Favorite Moment: _____
Notes: _____
_____

72

PLANTS VS. ZOMBIES

PLAY IT ON:
iOS, Android, PC, and more

GENRE:
Role Playing & Strategy

RATING:
E10+

FIRST SEEN:
2009

MADE BY:
PopCap Games

If there's one thing scarier than zombies, it's yard work. Be honest: would you rather fight off a hoard of the walking dead or spend all day planting petunias in your grandma's garden? If you don't mind either, you'll certainly enjoy the Plants vs. Zombies series.

Originally appearing on the PC in 2009, Plants vs. Zombies is a tower defense series that relies on quick thinking and a knowledge of super-powered greenery. The games, which rose to fame on the iPhone and iPad, are centered on stopping a slow-moving wave of zombies from invading a house. To do this, players must use their sun power to grow special plants and fungi that can keep the zombies at bay with seeds, explosions, and vicious bites. Not to be outdone, some zombies will suit up in homemade armor, jump on pogo sticks, and even get their boogie on to get into the house.

The sequel, *Plants vs. Zombies 2: It's About Time*, pits players against new zombies throughout history while offering powerful new plant friends. If you want to master this classic mobile strategy series, you'll have to use your delicious *brrrrraaaaaaaaiiiiinnnnnnssss.*

DID YOU KNOW?

In 2014, a spin-off game, *Garden Warfare* was launched. Unlike the original games, *Garden Warfare* puts players directly in control of both the plants and zombies in a third-person shooter frenzy.

Played it! ☐   My Rating: ☆☆☆☆☆
My Favorite Moment: _____
Notes: _____
_____

DRAGON QUEST

Classic games like checkers, horseshoes, and dominoes never go out of style. They stay true to their original look and feel even after decades have passed. The Dragon Quest series does the same in the world of video games. These traditional role-playing titles have been thrilling players for over 30 years, and each release captures a new generation of fans.

Famed *Dragon Ball* artist Akira Toriyama was commissioned to work on the Dragon Quest series, where his signature art style brings the many characters and monsters to life. Each adventure in the series follows a hero on a challenging quest to stop a powerful evil that is sweeping the land. As they progress through the main story of each game, heroes team up with allies who can assist in battle. Characters and their parties can travel to new locations on the large over world map, but must be wary of unseen enemies. When it's time to clash with enemy forces, party members must strategize the best form of attack.

The Dragon Quest series is well known for its monsters of every shape, size, and color. The most famous enemy is a wide-eyed blue blob known as a slime. If players encounter too many slimes, they may find themselves in a sticky situation.

DID YOU KNOW?

The Dragon Quest series is so popular that a full-sized controller in the shape of "slime" was released for the PlayStation 2. All the buttons and control sticks can be found on the slime's underside.

PLAY IT ON:
PS4, 3DS, DS, and more

GENRE:
Role Playing & Strategy

RATING:
E-T

FIRST SEEN:
1986

MADE BY:
Square Enix

Played it! ☐   My Rating: ☆☆☆☆☆
My Favorite Moment: _____
Notes: _____
_____

74

KINGDOM HEARTS

PLAY IT ON:
PS4, PS3, 3DS,
and more

GENRE:
Role Playing &
Strategy

RATING:
E-E 10+

**FIRST
SEEN:**
2002

MADE BY:
Square Enix

With series like Marvel vs. Capcom and Super Smash Bros., fans of gaming are no strangers to star-studded crossovers. One of the most unexpected team-ups came in the form of 2002's *Kingdom Hearts*, a role-playing title that features the heroes and villains of the popular Final Fantasy franchise and… the wonderful world of Disney.

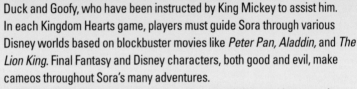

This unlikely journey starts with Sora, a young hero who finds himself in possession of the legendary Keyblade after his island is attacked by monsters known as the Heartless. Sora's close friends, Riku and Kairi, disappear in the aftermath, and he sets out to rescue them. Sora teams up with classic cartoon pals Donald Duck and Goofy, who have been instructed by King Mickey to assist him. In each Kingdom Hearts game, players must guide Sora through various Disney worlds based on blockbuster movies like *Peter Pan, Aladdin,* and *The Lion King*. Final Fantasy and Disney characters, both good and evil, make cameos throughout Sora's many adventures.

The Kingdom Hearts battle system includes real-time combat, meaning players must hack away at enemies while avoiding incoming blows. Traditional RPG elements like magic abilities and items can also be used to assist Sora or his party members. Think you can stop the Heartless and save the day? Be our guest.

DID YOU KNOW?

Original voice actress Kathryn Beaumont reprised her roles as Alice of *Alice in Wonderland* and Wendy Darling of *Peter Pan* for the Kingdom Hearts series after over 50 years had passed.

Played it! ☐ My Rating: ☆☆☆☆☆
My Favorite Moment: _____
Notes: _____
_____

PIKMIN

The world is a big place, and it's much bigger when you're less than an inch tall. You might not think a tree frog or a small puddle are anything to worry about, but to the tiny protagonists of the Pikmin series, these natural obstacles are an enormous problem.

When a comet collides with his spaceship, the miniature Captain Olimar finds himself stranded on an unknown planet filled with vegetation. Because oxygen is highly toxic to him, he must find all his ship parts and return to his home planet of Hocotate before his life support runs out. Olimar recruits small plant creatures known as Pikmin to help him. Each Pikmin has special abilities, such as being able to swim or being fire resistant. As more and more Pikmin join Olimar's colorful army, the more they can carry and the better they can fight. Players must be smart about where they send their Pikmin and for how long, as Pikmin are easily defeated and time is always ticking.

Every Pikmin game has introduced new pint-sized adventurers and new types of Pikmin for players to harvest. If you don't want your character pushing up daisies, you'll have to start pulling up Pikmin.

PLAY IT ON:
3DS, Wii U, Wii,
and more

GENRE:
Role Playing &
Strategy

RATING:
E-E10+

**FIRST
SEEN:**
2001

DID YOU KNOW?

Olimar's spaceship is titled the S.S. Dolphin. This is a nod to the code name for the GameCube, which was first announced as "Project Dolphin."

MADE BY:
Nintendo

Played it! ☐   My Rating: ☆☆☆☆☆
My Favorite Moment: _____
Notes: _____
_____

76

HEARTHSTONE

PLAY IT ON:
PC, iOS, and
Android

GENRE:
Role Playing &
Strategy

RATING:
T

**FIRST
SEEN:**
2014

MADE BY:
Blizzard

Traditional playing cards have been a popular way to pass the time, and in the early '90s, a new type of playing cards came on the scene. Collectible card games (CCG) or trading card games (TCG) involve starter decks that players purchase as an introduction to the gameplay with separate booster packs available to enhance a deck with more powerful cards. To build the best possible deck, players have to collect and trade cards.

In 2008, game developer Blizzard decided to put out a TCG based around their online smash hit *The World of Warcraft*. The card game ran for five years before Blizzard decided to discontinue it in favor of a new digital card game known as *Hearthstone: Heroes of Warcraft*. While *Hearthstone* is very similar to the physical TCGs it is based on, it gives players a free starter deck and lets them earn booster packs by winning matches. Players can also purchase booster packs within the game, which is a faster (but more expensive) way of beefing up their deck.

A match in *Hearthstone* is between two online players or one player and a computer opponent. Each player starts by picking a *Warcraft* hero and a deck that goes with their class. Powerful warlocks, sinister shamans, and brave warriors are just a few of the possible choices. To win a match, players must destroy their opponent's defense and bring their hit points down to zero by playing cards that cast spells, summon minions, and equip weapons. Matches are turn-based, so each side has time to strategize their next move.

The best part about *Hearthstone* is that the game will always help you when you're confused about what cards to play next. That means your little brother or sister can't cheat when you challenge them to a match.

DID YOU KNOW?

Each match in *Hearthstone* is played out on a game board with a special theme. Players can interact with certain spots on the game board—break the windows of a house, stroke a mythical griffin, or launch a catapult—all with a single tap.

30

THRALL

WHAT TO PLAY NEXT:
Pokémon TCG Online
Adventure Time: Card Wars
Duelyst

TOP CARD PACK PICKS:
Whispers of the Old Gods
Mean Streets of Gadgetzan
Journey to Un'Goro

YOU'LL LIKE THESE GAMES IF...
You always have a card
up your sleeve.

Played it! ☐ My Rating: ☆☆☆☆☆
My Favorite Moment: _____
Notes: _____
_____

77

NI NO KUNI

GENRE:
Role Playing &
Strategy

RATING:
E10+

**FIRST
SEEN:**
2010

MADE BY:
Level-5

If you have ever wanted to be a wizard, the Ni no Kuni games should be your first stop. The original *Ni no Kuni* title launched in Japan for the Nintendo DS and was later updated for the PS3 as *Ni no Kuni: Wrath of the White Witch*. The enchanting character design and animation for the series come from the world-renowned Studio Ghibli, creators of classic anime movies like *My Neighbor Totoro, Spirited Away,* and *Ponyo.*

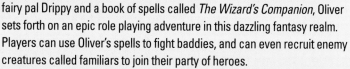

Wrath of the White Witch centers on Oliver, a young boy who must travel to Ni no Kuni, or another world, to save his mother after she passes away. With the help of his fairy pal Drippy and a book of spells called *The Wizard's Companion*, Oliver sets forth on an epic role playing adventure in this dazzling fantasy realm. Players can use Oliver's spells to fight baddies, and can even recruit enemy creatures called familiars to join their party of heroes.

The most recent title, *Ni no Kuni II: Revenant Kingdom*, follows a new protagonist, King Evan Pettiwhisker Tildrum. Whether you're controlling Oliver or King Evan, the Ni no Kuni series will surely work its magic on you.

DID YOU KNOW?

Players who preordered a special edition of *Ni no Kuni: Wrath of the White Witch* received a life-sized printed version of *The Wizard's Companion*. This 340-page book includes chapters on magic, alchemy, armor, and more.

Played it! ☐ My Rating: ☆☆☆☆☆

My Favorite Moment: _____

Notes: _____

_____

POKÉMON MYSTERY DUNGEON

Pokémon trainers the world over know the excitement that comes with catching, trading, and battling an ever-growing roster of monsters. But what is it like to actually *be* a Pokémon? The Pokémon Mystery Dungeon series gives players the opportunity to find out.

In each Pokémon Mystery Dungeon adventure, players take the role of a human who has been transformed into a Pokémon with no memory. The Pokémon a player can choose to be varies depending on the game; there are classic starters like Pikachu, Totodile, and Snivy, with many more available. At the beginning of the journey, a familiar friend shows players the basics of being a wild Pokémon, from how to attack an opponent to how to heal with items.

The Pokémon Mystery Dungeon series falls under the dungeon crawler category of role-playing games. This means players spend most of their time navigating maze-like environments with a team of friends, fighting off opponents, and rescuing those in need. Each of the dungeons is randomly generated, which means you could play any of the games 100 times, and it would always be different.

When asked about the series, Pikachu says, "Pika, Pika. Pikachu!" which translates to, "It's one of my favorites. You should definitely try it!"

PLAY IT ON:
3DS, DS, and GB

GENRE:
Role Playing & Strategy

RATING:
E

FIRST SEEN:
2005

DID YOU KNOW?

Though you can only pick from certain Pokémon to be your main character, *Pokémon Super Mystery Dungeon* for the 3DS features over 700 Pokémon to interact with. At least you don't have to catch them all this time, right?

MADE BY:
Nintendo

Played it! ☐　My Rating: ☆☆☆☆☆

My Favorite Moment: _____

Notes: _____

_____

TETRIS

During the 1980's, the United States and the Soviet Union were not the best of friends. It was during this time, known as The Cold War, that a software engineer living in the Soviet Union named Alexey Pajitnov created *Tetris*. The name *Tetris* is a combination of the prefix *tetra* meaning four (because the blocks, or *tetrominos*, are made of four sections), and popular racquet sport tennis.

PLAY IT ON:
Switch, PS4, iOS, and more

GENRE:
Puzzle & Arcade

RATING:
E

FIRST SEEN:
1984

MADE BY:
The Tetris Company

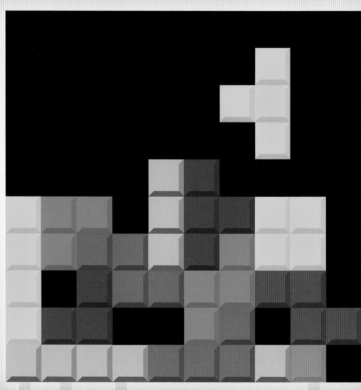

DID YOU KNOW?

A trilogy of sci-fi *Tetris* movies has been announced for release in the near future. Gaming fans are curious about what the movie's plot will center on.

Pajitnov didn't create *Tetris* to make money; he just enjoyed building fun games in his spare time. After his work friends passed it around, the puzzle game made its way to a software exhibit and was eventually picked up by a gaming distributor. Despite the Cold War, *Tetris* still launched in the United States to great success. Nintendo bundled it with their original Game Boy system, introducing it to millions of players around the world.

Classic *Tetris* gameplay is focused on falling blocks that can be moved and spun to fit into different areas. Using the game's seven types of tetrominos, players must attempt to fill in a complete row with no gaps, and clear enough rows to move to the next level. The thrill of *Tetris* comes from its randomly generated stream of blocks and increasing speed.

Over the years, there have been dozens of different versions of *Tetris* that feature everything from 3D blocks to never-ending marathon modes. The most recent *Tetris* spin-off is *Puyo Puyo Tetris*, a game where players can switch back and forth between two puzzle classics and even go head-to-head with a buddy. With such simple and addicting gameplay, it's no surprise that *Tetris* is the best selling gaming series of all time with almost 500 million copies sold.

WHAT TO PLAY NEXT:
The Dr. Mario series
The Puyo Puyo series
Pokémon Puzzle Challenge

TOP SERIES PICKS:
Tetris (GB, 1989)
Tetris DS (DS, 2006)
Puyo Puyo Tetris
(PS4, Switch, 2017)

YOU'LL LIKE THESE GAMES IF...
You have the fastest mind on the block.

Played it! ☐   My Rating: ☆☆☆☆☆

My Favorite Moment: _____

Notes: _____

_____

PAC-MAN

PLAY IT ON:
Switch, PS4,
XOne, and more

GENRE:
Puzzle &
Arcade

RATING:
E

**FIRST
SEEN:**
1980

MADE BY:
Bandai Namco

Pac-Man is possibly gaming's greatest icon. Not only does he predate most other gaming heroes, Pac-Man has always been widely regarded as a series anyone can pick up and play. In fact, Pac-Man creator Toru Iwatani was sick of arcade titles focused on war and wanted to build a game that appealed to both male and female gamers of any age. It's safe to say he succeeded.

DID YOU KNOW?
In the original *Pac-Man*, you can get a score so high that it actually breaks the game. If you can get past 3,333,360 points, you may be lucky enough to see what is known as a kill screen.
Good luck with that!

Legend has it Pac-Man's design came from a pizza that was missing a slice, while his name was inspired by the Japanese onomatopoeia (a word that sounds like what it's describing) *Paku-Paku*. The noise mimics the opening and closing of a mouth. Say *Paku-Paku* a few times out loud and you'll see what we mean.

The average game of Pac-Man drops players into the middle of a brightly colored maze filled with white pellets. Players must navigate Pac-Man through this neon labyrinth to eat every single pellet before getting caught by the four pesky wandering ghosts. Each ghost has a different color and personality, meaning experienced players can tell exactly where the ghosts will go. The only way to defeat these pixelated spirits is to eat a Power Pellet, a large glowing dot found in the corners of each maze. Once Pac-Man gets a hold of one of these, it's ghost gobbling time!

Over the years, the Pac-Man series has tried many different styles of gameplay. Titles like *Ms. Pac-Man* and *Pac-Man Championship Edition* have stayed true to the arcade roots, but the Namco mascot has also been featured as a platforming hero, a fighting game brawler, and more.

The world is always hungry for a new take on classic Pac-Man action. Waka Waka!

WHAT TO PLAY NEXT:
Dig Dug
Q*bert
Frogger

TOP SERIES PICKS:
Pac-Man (Arcade, 1981)
Pac-Man World 2
(PS2, GC, Xbox, 2004)
Pac-Man Championship Edition 2
(PS4, XOne, PC, 2016)

YOU'LL LIKE THESE GAMES IF...
You're always hungry!

Played it! ☐   My Rating: ☆☆☆☆☆
My Favorite Moment: _____
Notes: _____
_____

81

KATAMARI

PLAY IT ON:
PSVita, PS3, PS2,
and more

GENRE:
Puzzle &
Arcade

RATING:
E–E10+

**FIRST
SEEN:**
2004

MADE BY:
Bandai Namco

Everyone has that one relative who's just a bit weird. The main character of the Katamari games is no exception. His father, The King of All Cosmos, is one strange fellow. He is known for his dramatic speeches and wonderfully bizarre outfits.

The Katamari series is one of a kind. When the King of All Cosmos demands more stars and constellations be added to the sky, his son, the Prince, must lend a hand. To help, the Prince must push a katamari (Japanese for *clump*) around different environments, slowly rolling up and collecting various items. The more items you collect, the bigger the ball gets, and the more items you can roll over. Everything, from paper clips to killer whales, is fair game when the Prince is on a roll. Collect enough junk in one katamari, and The King of All Cosmos will send it into the heavens to become a new part of the night sky.

The Prince's katamari technique works well for his crazy adventures, but it sadly can't be used to clean up your room. However, this truly unique puzzle game will have you snorting with laughter and shaking your head in amazement.

DID YOU KNOW?

Both the Prince and the King of All Cosmos were originally going to be characters in a driving game where players would attempt to crash into as many obstacles as possible.

Played it! ☐ My Rating: ☆☆☆☆☆
My Favorite Moment: _____
Notes: _____
_____

GALAGA

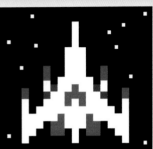

When the galaxy is threatened by a swarm of alien insects, there's only one thing to do—blast those pesky space bugs with your intergalactic star fighter! The more enemies you hit, the higher your score, but it only gets harder as you dodge and shoot your way through each oncoming wave.

The original 1981 *Galaga* arcade title is actually the sequel to another game known as *Galaxian*. While *Galaxian* is a hit in its own right, *Galaga* took the spotlight due to its improved gameplay, audio, and graphics. Players take control of a laser-firing star fighter and maneuver it from side to side, attempting to shoot down a screen full of alien intruders. The enemies in *Galaga* are famous for their variety of attacks; certain insects dive-bomb your ship, and others attempt to catch you in their expanding tractor beam. It takes some quick thinking and a whole lot of lasers to take down these space baddies.

Like *Pac-Man* and other arcade classics, the Galaga series has been remixed and rereleased on many different platforms. In 2016, *Galaga Wars* launched for iOS and Android devices with all new touch controls, explosive power-ups, and loads of tricky enemies. The fate of the galaxy is literally at your fingertips.

PLAY IT ON:
iOS, Android, 3DS, and more

GENRE:
Puzzle & Arcade

RATING:
E

FIRST SEEN:
1981

DID YOU KNOW?

In the superhero blockbuster *The Avengers*, Tony Stark (Iron Man) catches one of the S.H.I.E.L.D. agents playing *Galaga* when he should be working. Whoops!

MADE BY:
Bandai Namco

Played it! ☐   My Rating: ☆☆☆☆☆

My Favorite Moment: _____

Notes: _____

_____

83

DUCK HUNT

PLAY IT ON:
Wii U and NES

GENRE:
Puzzle &
Arcade

RATING:
E

**FIRST
SEEN:**
1984

MADE BY:
Nintendo

In 1976, Nintendo released *Beam Gun: Duck Hunt,* an electronic toy that featured a small projector and a plastic gun. Flying ducks were projected on a wall, and owners would use their handy beam gun to try and shoot them down.

However, the *Duck Hunt* that most gamers know is the NES version, which came with a beam gun of its own called the NES Zapper. A cartridge that contained both *Super Mario Bros.* and *Duck Hunt* was bundled with the NES "Action Set" when it launched in North America.

The gameplay of *Duck Hunt* is very reminiscent of an arcade title. Players attempt to shoot down as many ducks as they can to improve their overall score. But beware—if you let a duck fly away, you'll be face to face with the smug mug and soul-shattering laughter of the infamous *Duck Hunt* dog. The NES classic even has a multiplayer mode. By plugging in a second controller, another player can control the flight path of the ducks, attempting to escape the hunter.

DID YOU KNOW?

The NES version of *Duck Hunt* can't be played properly on any HDTV. Sadly, the old-school technology in the NES Zapper can't recognize the digital display of modern TVs. Good thing you can still play it on the Wii U's virtual console!

Played it! ☐   My Rating: ☆☆☆☆☆
My Favorite Moment: _____
Notes: _____
_____

THREES

Threes is known as the "tiny puzzle that grows on you." Players begin with a random assortment of numbered cards on a four by four grid. To advance the game, players must swipe together similar numbers, as well as ones and twos, to rack up a new high score. Two sixes combine to make a twelve, two twelves become a twenty-four, and so on. It's only game over when the grid is filled, and you can't combine any more cards. That's it! It may seem overly simple, but that's the beauty of *Threes*. It's a game anyone can pick up and play at a moment's notice.

    Threes' fluid gameplay is surrounded by adorable card characters and catchy background melodies. Each card has a tiny face that looks excitedly at similar cards and will shout out to the player if combined with its twin. The first time players reach a new high number, that number's card character appears with a short introduction. Discover cards like Threejay (192), who has pointy fangs, and Terrace (1,536), who has spider legs. Legend has it there's a special card at 12,288… but you'll just have to find out.

PLAY IT ON:
XOne, iOS, and Android

GENRE:
Puzzle & Arcade

RATING:
E

FIRST SEEN:
2014

DID YOU KNOW?

Threes players who manage to produce a 768 card are introduced to the bloodthirsty card character Triferatu. "Tri" is a prefix that means three, and "feratu" is a reference to famous silent film vampire Nosferatu. Spooky!

MADE BY:
Sirvo

Played it! ☐   My Rating: ☆☆☆☆☆

My Favorite Moment: _____

Notes: _____

_____

85

PORTAL

PLAY IT ON:
PC, XOne, PS3,
and more

GENRE:
Puzzle &
Arcade

RATING:
E10+-T

**FIRST
SEEN:**
2007

MADE BY:
Valve

Taking a test can be stressful—especially a pop quiz! Now imagine waking up in a strange lab, and your test is to survive different trials using new, radical technology.

The Portal series opens with such a scenario. Test subject Chell is told she must wield Aperture Labs' newest invention, the portal gun, as she works to find her way out of various test chambers. GLaDOS, a robotic being who is programmed throughout the entire lab, gives instructions and warnings to Chell. As Chell advances, GLaDOS promises she will be rewarded with cake if she manages to complete the entire portal test. It's only after Chell finds some troubling messages claiming "The cake is a lie," that she realizes GLaDOS may be up to something more sinister.

The gameplay of the original *Portal* title is like nothing the world of puzzle gaming had ever seen. From a first-person perspective, players control Chell to create two linked portals on various surfaces—a blue portal and an orange portal—to get through obstacles. If you need to jump over a large gap, simply shoot portals—one onto the opposite wall and one at your feet—and hop through to make it across! While this sounds like a very simple mechanic, you must get very creative with portal placement and in-game physics to survive every trial.

The sequel to *Portal*, unsurprisingly named *Portal 2*, has even more tricks up its sleeve, including special gels and a cooperative campaign. You'll have to play them both if you want to experience the complete Portal story. Plus, if you beat both games, we'll totally give you some delicious cake...

DID YOU KNOW?

The Portal series began as a student project called *Narbacular Drop*, a game where players attempted to escape a dungeon by using portals. Valve was so impressed with the project that they hired the whole development team.

WHAT TO PLAY NEXT:
Quantum Conundrum
The Talos Principle
Q.U.B.E.

TOP SERIES PICKS:
Portal (PC, PS3, X360, 2007)
Portal: Still Alive (X360, 2008)
Portal 2 (PC, PS3, X360, 2011)

YOU'LL LIKE THESE GAMES IF...
You have always wanted to be
two places at once.

Played it! ☐   My Rating: ☆☆☆☆☆

My Favorite Moment: _____

Notes: _____

_____

86

DR. MARIO

PLAY IT ON:
Wii U, 3DS, Wii,
and more

GENRE:
Puzzle &
Arcade

RATING:
E

**FIRST
SEEN:**
1990

MADE BY:
Nintendo

AH-CHOO! Oh dear, it seems you've come down with a nasty cold. Never fear, Dr. Mario is here to put those pesky germs in their place.

Not satisfied with just being a plumber, Mario moved into medicine with the debut of *Dr. Mario* for the NES. The game features Mario throwing colorful pills, called Megavitamins, into a giant bottle to eradicate different viruses. Each pill is split in two, with the possibility of red, blue, or yellow sections. Much like *Tetris*, players must rotate and maneuver Dr. Mario's falling pills to drop them in just the right spot. Once a virus comes in contact with three pill sections of the same color, it is momentarily destroyed. As players progress through the different stages, more and more viruses pop up. If the bottle overflows with pills before players can wipe out the viruses, it's game over.

Mario isn't the only one prescribing puzzling vaccines. In 2013, *Dr. Luigi* was released for the Wii U, and the brothers teamed up in the most recent title *Dr. Mario: Miracle Cure* for the 3DS. Just be thankful you haven't had to visit Dr. Bowser. That guy definitely didn't go to medical school.

DID YOU KNOW?

A prototype of the first *Dr. Mario* shows the game was originally called *Virus* and featured Mario curing a sick dog. The poor pooch can be seen sneezing as Mario lines up his pills.

Played it! ☐ My Rating: ☆☆☆☆☆
My Favorite Moment: _____
Notes: _____
_____

PICROSS

If you took a magnifying glass and looked closely at the average TV or computer screen, you would see teeny, tiny squares of color, or pixels. As technology has advanced, pixels have become smaller and more defined, making games and movies look much clearer and sharper. But every image, no matter how detailed, can be broken down into these little squares.

Picross is the puzzle series that has players filling in pixels on a grid one by one to slowly reveal a full picture. Number clues on the sides of the grid help to figure out which squares need to be filled. If a row has the number five next to it, then five of the pixels in that row will need to be filled to complete the image. Multiple numbers indicate a break between filled-in squares, which can make things tricky when trying to line them all up perfectly.

3DS owners can find both old and new Picross games for Nintendo series like Mario, Zelda, and Pokémon in the handheld's eShop, while those who truly want a challenge should try their hand at *Picross 3D: Round 2*. They say the best things come in small packages, so point yourself in the direction of some Picross pixel perfection!

PLAY IT ON:
3DS, DS, GB, and more

GENRE:
Puzzle & Arcade

RATING:
E

FIRST SEEN:
1995

MADE BY:
Jupiter/ Nintendo

DID YOU KNOW?

The first Picross game was *Mario's Picross* for the original Game Boy. The game features Mario as an archaeologist who uses a hammer and chisel to carve out each square on the puzzle grid.

Played it! ☐   My Rating: ☆☆☆☆☆

My Favorite Moment: _____

Notes: _____
_____

88

ANGRY BIRDS

PLAY IT ON:
iOS, Android,
3DS, and more

GENRE:
Puzzle &
Arcade

RATING:
E

**FIRST
SEEN:**
2009

MADE BY:
Rovio

Birds can be very territorial animals—they don't like it when humans or other animals get too close to their nests or babies. So it's no surprise that the stars of *Angry Birds* got a bit upset when a group of sickly green swine took off with all their precious eggs. To get revenge on those naughty piggies, the birds attack with a giant slingshot.

By pulling back on the bird in the slingshot, players can angle the birds to fly right into the weakest points of the crudely built pig fortresses. Upon release, the birds give a mighty chirp of rebellion as they smash into walls, boulders, and enemies. Once all the pigs in a stage have been destroyed, players are given a star rating and access to the next showdown.

As players progress, they get access to an arsenal of aviary allies. There are nine types of playable birds (and many more in recent games) for players to use, each with their own special powers. These birds have unique shapes and colors so players can tell just what kind of winged weaponry they are dealing with. Yellow canary Chuck can crank up his speed mid-flight for some serious damage. Jay, Jake, and Jim, a trio of blue birds, can split in the air to hit multiple objects at once. It's important to know how a bird attacks and where to sling it, especially for harder stages.

The Angry Birds franchise is one of the most popular mobile series in history, with oodles of spin-offs and even a full-length animated movie. Games like *Angry Birds Seasons* and *Angry Birds Space* have featured new environments and enhanced gameplay that fans of the series can master. The next time you wake up to a bird chirping outside your window, you may just want to cover your head and go back to sleep!

DID YOU KNOW?

In 2011, Angry Birds developer Rovio revealed that players were putting in 300 MILLION minutes of combined play every single day. That's roughly 570 years worth of time spent launching birds in just 24 hours!

WHAT TO PLAY NEXT:
Crush the Castle 2
Cut the Rope
World of Goo

TOP SERIES PICKS:
Angry Birds (iOS, 2009)
Angry Birds: Star Wars II
   (iOS, Android, 2013)
Angry Birds 2 (iOS, Android, 2015)

YOU'LL LIKE THESE GAMES IF...
You have eggcellent aim.

Played it! ☐   My Rating: ☆☆☆☆☆

My Favorite Moment: _____

Notes: _____

_____

89

BOXBOY!

PLAY IT ON:
3DS

GENRE:
Puzzle &
Arcade

RATING:
E

**FIRST
SEEN:**
2015

MADE BY:
Nintendo

The developers at HAL Laboratory are famous for creating and developing the Kirby series (see page 10), a line of platforming titles known for their adorably simple hero and his floaty gameplay. What could they possibly create that's more basic than a pink ball with red shoes? The answer: A box. Well, not just any box, a BoxBoy!

The BoxBoy! series is a mix of both puzzle gameplay and platforming—players must use their smarts to overcome increasingly difficult obstacles. The game's hero, a black and white box by the name of Qbby, must use his box-creating ability to solve each puzzling challenge.

Qbby can push boxes (the maximum number varies in each stage) from the right, left, or top of his body to use as bridges and barriers to avoid bottomless pits, pointy spikes, and deadly lasers. Players who manage to guide him to the end of each stage are rewarded with medals, which can be used to purchase new outfits, special challenges, and groovy music. This is one puzzle game where you're going to have to think both inside *and* outside the box.

DID YOU KNOW?

Some of the costumes players can unlock in the BoxBoy! series include ninja, bunny, robot, superhero, rapper, kitty cat, and more. Qbby is always looking fresh to death!

Played it! ☐   My Rating: ☆☆☆☆☆
My Favorite Moment: _____
Notes: _____
_____

PUSHMO

90

When push comes to shove, some puzzle games are just more fun than others. The Pushmo series (known as Pullblox in Europe) is certainly one of the best.

In the original *Pushmo* title, players are introduced to Mallo, a chubby red creature who resembles a sumo wrestler. While spending the day in Pushmo Park, Mallo is recruited by Papa Blox to save some children who have gotten themselves stranded on top of the colorful Pushmo puzzle structures. To rescue these roly-poly youngsters, Mallo must push and pull different sliding blocks of the structures so he can form a path to the top. The blocks can only be pulled out up to three lengths, so players have to ponder just how far in or out to arrange them. Once Mallo reaches the trapped tot, he can move on to the next tricky Pushmo puzzle. Some of the structures in the park are just blocky bits, while others resemble actual images.

Mallo returns for further puzzle-solving fun in the 3DS exclusives *Crashmo* and *Stretchmo*, both of which feature new perplexing block mechanics. Both *Pushmo* and *Pushmo World* for Wii U let players build and share their own push and pull puzzles. Don't be a square, give the Pushmo series a try!

PLAY IT ON:
Wii U and 3DS

GENRE:
Puzzle & Arcade

RATING:
E

FIRST SEEN:
2011

MADE BY:
Nintendo

DID YOU KNOW?

Since all the puzzles in the Pushmo series are made of blocks, Nintendo decided to include some stages based on classic pixelated characters like Mario, Link, Samus, and more.

Played it! ☐   My Rating: ☆☆☆☆☆
My Favorite Moment: _____
Notes: _____

91

PROFESSOR LAYTON

PLAY IT ON:
3DS, DS, iOS,
and more

GENRE:
Puzzle &
Arcade

RATING:
E-T

**FIRST
SEEN:**
2007

MADE BY:
Level-5

When there is trouble afoot and mysteries to be solved, there's only one man to call: Sherlock Hol- wait, no, that's not it. Ah yes, that's right. It's Professor Hershel Layton! Even though he's just a professor of archaeology at London's Gressenheller University, he's still unmatched when it comes to unraveling puzzles of all sorts. With his signature top hat and sidekick Luke, he can take on any challenge, no matter how bewildering or mysterious.

The Professor Layton series has long been the go-to franchise for gamers who want fascinating logic puzzles with a dash of English wit. When introduced to a new environment, players must poke around to uncover a new mystery for the professor to decipher. Anything is a puzzle in the world of Professor Layton—haircuts, bookshelves, sandwiches, match sticks, toy cars, and more. Some of these puzzles are important to the main plot of each game, while others are simply bonus challenges for those who truly want to become a super sleuth.

When solving a puzzle, players must use the given clues and logical thinking to find a suitable answer. A player can choose to use a handy hint coin, but beware! Players can only use so many hint coins before they're forced to make the next deduction on their own.

Once certain puzzles have been solved, players are given items to use in Professor Layton's enormous trunk. These items are part of a meta puzzle, or a puzzle that can only be completed by using parts of other puzzles. Only the smartest of the smart can put together these unusual items to unlock the secrets of Layton's trunk.

After seven games and hundreds of mysteries, a peculiar thing happened to the brilliant professor—he vanished! In the latest title, *Layton's Mystery Journey: Katrielle and the Millionaires' Conspiracy*, players must assist the Professor's daughter, Katrielle "Kat" Layton, as she searches for her missing father. Maybe he got locked in his own trunk; you'll just have to play and find out.

DID YOU KNOW?

Every puzzle in the series gives players the option of using hint coins… except one. A special puzzle known as "*The Diabolical Box Reopened*" in *Professor Layton and the Unwound Future* features no hints whatsoever. How curious!

WHAT TO PLAY NEXT:
Ghost Trick: Phantom Detective
Puzzle Agent
The Witness

TOP SERIES PICKS:
Professor Layton and the Curious Village (DS, 2007)
Professor Layton and the Unwound Future (DS, 2008)
Professor Layton and the Azran Legacy (3DS, 2013)

YOU'LL LIKE THESE GAMES IF...
You have a sense for sleuthing.

Played it! ☐ My Rating: ☆☆☆☆☆

My Favorite Moment: _____

Notes: _____

_____

GAME NO.

92

MARIO PARTY

PLAY IT ON:
Wii U, 3DS, Wii,
and more

GENRE:
Party &
Rhythm

RATING:
E

**FIRST
SEEN:**
1998

MADE BY:
Nintendo

You probably have been to a birthday party, but there's nothing quite like a Mario Party. While other parties have guests stuffing their faces with cake and ice cream or swinging blindly at a candy-filled piñata, a Mario Party involves jumping rope with fire, outrunning ghosts, and tracing pictures with

DID YOU KNOW?

In *Mario Party 10* for the Wii U, players can select Bowser Party mode where a fifth player can play as Bowser using the Wii U gamepad to try to ruin everyone's fun. RAWR!

130

a jackhammer. You can see why some might find it a bit more exciting than the average get-together.

The first *Mario Party* game was introduced on the Nintendo 64. The N64's multiple controller ports were perfect for a game about hanging out with friends for some multiplayer madness. In the original title, players pick a themed game board and select Mario or one of his pals as their character. Each turn involves players rolling the die, choosing where on the board to move, and attempting to nab one of the shiny Power Stars. After all players have moved, they must compete in a random mini-game to earn coins and other helpful items.

One of the best parts about the Mario Party games is that you never know which mini-game you'll be playing or how many characters will be on each team. You could be in a free-for-all fishing contest or end up in a 2-on-2 bobsled race. At the end of the game, it's all about who has the most Power Stars, and players must do whatever it takes to earn, buy, and steal as many as they can before time runs out.

As the Mario Party series has evolved over the years, it has introduced hundreds of new mini-games, dozens of creative game boards, and a handful of interesting changes to the main party mode. For example, *Mario Party 10* for the Wii U features both motion and touch controls, as well as a vehicle system where all players stay together as they move across the game board. Partying will never be the same.

WHAT TO PLAY NEXT:
Nintendo Land
Wii Party U
1-2-Switch

TOP SERIES PICKS:
Mario Party 2 (N64, 1999)
Mario Party 3 (N64, 2000)
Mario Party Star Rush (3DS, 2016)

YOU'LL LIKE THESE GAMES IF...
You're always the life of the party!

Played it! ☐   My Rating: ☆☆☆☆☆☆

My Favorite Moment: _____

Notes: _____

_____

93

PATAPON

PLAY IT ON:
PS4, PSVita,
and PSP

GENRE:
Party &
Rhythm

RATING:
E

**FIRST
SEEN:**
2007

MADE BY:
Pyramid/SCE
Japan Studio

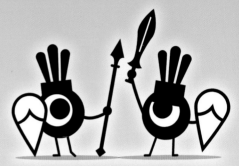

Pata-Pata-Pata-Pon! It may sound like an overly excited marching band, but it's actually the chant of fearless miniature warriors on their way into battle. Only you, the Almighty, can control their next move and lead them to victory.

The Patapon series is a trio of rhythm games like no other. Instead of repeating back a string of beats or trying to hit certain incoming notes on time, players must create their own musical masterpiece based on what they want their army of one-eyed soldiers to do next. Each of the main four PlayStation face buttons are used to control a different ancient war drum. The four drums each have their own distinct sound, which are heard as *Pata*, *Pon*, *Chaka*, and *Don*. By staying on rhythm and using different combinations of these drum beats, players can tell their tribe of loyal warriors to advance, fight, retreat, and defend.

Before each mission, players can beef up their Patapon horde with new recruits and an arsenal of tiny weapons. Only when you've mastered the rhythm of the war drums and collected enough troops can you beat back your enemies and beat up the beat. *Pon-Pon-Pata-Pon!*

DID YOU KNOW?

The drums in the Patapon series are inspired by West African talking drums. These flexible instruments use a special pitch and tone to make sounds that resemble a person talking or humming.

Played it! ☐ My Rating: ☆☆☆☆☆

My Favorite Moment: _____

Notes: _____
_____

RHYTHM HEAVEN

Music and rhythm can be found everywhere, whether it's the babbling of a stream, the thwack of a ping-pong paddle, or the majestic chomp of a bear eating donuts. Wait... what was that last one?

The Rhythm Heaven series (known as Rhythm Paradise in Europe) began life as a Japan-only Game Boy Advance title. The game was so quirky and loved by fans that the second title was released worldwide for the Nintendo DS. Two more installments have been released over the years, one for Wii and the other for 3DS.

Rhythm Heaven games are made up of dozens and dozens of individual rhythm levels, each with their own settings, characters, and controls. After a brief tutorial on when and how to stay on beat, players must try their hand at keeping time and staying with the level's unique rhythm. The individual stages in Rhythm Heaven are well-known for putting players in bizarre and distracting situations, such as playing badminton between two airplanes, trimming stray hairs off an onion, translating alien languages, and shooting nosy ghosts with a bow and arrow. There is no telling what nutty task you'll be asked to do next, but you can be sure it'll have your toes tapping.

PLAY IT ON:
3DS, Wii, and DS

GENRE:
Party &
Rhythm

RATING:
E

FIRST SEEN:
2006

MADE BY:
Nintendo

DID YOU KNOW?

All the original developers took a dance class together to gain a better understanding of rhythm. It was difficult, but it helped them find the right groove for the game.

Played it! ☐   My Rating: ☆☆☆☆☆
My Favorite Moment: _____
Notes: _____
_____

95

WARIOWARE

PLAY IT ON:
Wii U, Wii, DS,
and more

GENRE:
Party &
Rhythm

RATING:
E-E10+

**FIRST
SEEN:**
2003

MADE BY:
Nintendo

Pew! Do you smell that? It smells like… garlic and greed. That, my friend, is the smell of the diabolical Wario. Although he's mainly known for his go-karting skills and his bizarre moves in the Smash Bros. series, the elfish fiend was originally created to be the ultimate rival for Mario.

Wario made his debut in *Super Mario Land 2* for the Game Boy as the game's main villain. Since then he has gone on to star in his own adventure games, and has made cameo appearances in a variety of other Nintendo titles. While Wario games have always been a bit more unusual than your average video game romp, it's the WarioWare series that is truly his weirdest legacy.

Most gamers have played their fair share of minigames, but the WarioWare titles take this concept to the next level with *microgames*, or quick bursts of random action with few instructions that only last a few seconds. *Jump! Catch! Dodge!* In WarioWare, you'll only survive if you can react in time.

The WarioWare series features many zany characters in addition to Wario who have their own collections of microgames, including mad scientist Dr. Crygor, magical witch Ashley, and retro game fan 9-Volt. Players can fail up to three times before they are forced to start again from the beginning of a collection. If they manage to pass a certain number of microgames, they'll reach special boss stages and face even faster challenges.

There's no telling what kind of hilarious task you'll be asked to complete when it comes to WarioWare. Tickling an armpit, jumping over a potato, and transforming into a superhero are just a few of the hundreds of microgames featured. There are even some collections based on classic Nintendo franchises, such as *Duck Hunt, F-Zero,* and *The Legend of Zelda.* If you like picking games, and games where you can pick a virtual nose, then you'll be right at home with the WarioWare series.

DID YOU KNOW?

Super Smash Bros. Brawl for the Wii introduced a stage called "WarioWare Inc." where fighters must battle while performing random actions like sidestepping arrows, chiseling a statue, and trying to stay under an umbrella.

WHAT TO PLAY NEXT:
The Mario Party series
The Rhythm Heaven series
The Wario Land series

TOP SERIES PICKS:
WarioWare, Inc.:
Mega Microgames! (GB, 2003)
WarioWare: Touched! (DS, 2005)
WarioWare: Smooth Moves
(Wii, 2007)

YOU'LL LIKE THESE GAMES IF...
You have a short attention span.
Hey look, a squirrel!

Played it! ☐   My Rating: ☆☆☆☆☆

My Favorite Moment: _____

Notes: _____
_____

96

ROCK BAND

PLAY IT ON:
PS4, XOne, PS3,
and more

GENRE:
Party &
Rhythm

RATING:
E-T

**FIRST
SEEN:**
2007

MADE BY:
Harmonix

Learning to play an instrument can be difficult and buying one can be expensive. Good thing you don't have to be a millionaire to rock out in the virtual world! The Rock Band series has been giving players the opportunity to live out their rock 'n' roll dreams for the last decade.

Rock Band developer Harmonix began their video game career by creating the sci-fi themed rhythm titles *Frequency* and *Amplitude*. Both were loved by players and critics, but failed to sell very well. After finding

DID YOU KNOW?

In 2009, Harmonix teamed up with LEGO® to produce *LEGO® Rock Band*. The game lets players build their own band of LEGO® minifigures and switches out the normal incoming notes with glowing LEGO® bricks.

a hit with a singing series Karaoke Revolution, Harmonix worked with company RedOctane to develop a whole new type of music title with a special guitar controller. This game was eventually released as *Guitar Hero*, the smash success that started the interactive rhythm revolution on home consoles. Harmonix then began to work on a similar title that included more than just guitars—*Rock Band*.

WHAT TO PLAY NEXT:
Amplitude
Guitar Hero Live
Dance Dance Revolution

The first Rock Band title included lead guitar, bass guitar, vocals, and drums. The game was bundled with small plastic versions of a single Stratocaster guitar, a drum kit, and a microphone. Gameplay in the Rock Band series is based on hitting different colored notes that appear on screen and scroll toward the player. Players have to hold down a specific button on their guitar controller and strum at the right time to score points and keep their note streak alive. Drummers do the same by hitting the correct drum pad, and singers must change their pitch to stay in tune with the current lyrics.

TOP SERIES PICKS:
The Beatles: Rock Band
(PS3, X360, Wii, 2009)
Rock Band 3 (PS3, X360, Wii, 2010)
Rock Band 4 (PS4, XOne, 2015)

Hundreds of songs by famous bands and solo artists have been featured in the Rock Band series, including Aerosmith, Metallica, The Who, Maroon 5, Lady Gaga, and Bruno Mars. Special stand-alone versions of Rock Band have been released that focus solely on punk rockers Green Day and classic rock superstars The Beatles. There is plenty of music from every genre and decade for music lovers young and old to enjoy. So break out the fingerless gloves and put on your cheetah print headband—it's time to rock!

YOU'LL LIKE THESE GAMES IF...
You play air guitar to every song you hear.

Played it! ☐   My Rating: ☆☆☆☆☆

My Favorite Moment: _____

Notes: _____

_____

PARAPPA THE RAPPER

PLAY IT ON:
PS4, PS3, PS2,
and more

GENRE:
Party &
Rhythm

RATING:
E

**FIRST
SEEN:**
1996

MADE BY:
NanaOn-Sha

If you like fresh beats and creative rap, just look for the dog in the orange knit cap. He can take any everyday situation and turn it into a hip-hop demonstration. He's Parappa the Rapper, and you better believe that it's rhythm and rhymes that he's here to achieve!

The world of rhythm games has grown a lot in the past two decades, but Parappa the Rapper led the way with his 1996 PlayStation release.

DID YOU KNOW?
A spin-off to the Parappa the Rapper series was released in 1999 called *Um Jammer Lammy*. The PlayStation game keeps the Parappa series cartoon look and rhythm gameplay, but focuses on the rock music of lamb guitarist Lammy.

The title is said to be the first modern music video game and predates classics such as *Dance Dance Revolution, Samba de Amigo,* and *Guitar Hero*. The original Parappa title introduced the core rhythm concept of correctly timing lyrics and beats to line up with icons on screen. Though there have only been two official Parappa the Rapper titles (and two remakes), the games have earned a cult following by die-hard rhythm fanatics.

Parappa games are split into multiple song stages, each one featuring a different theme and rap master, such as kung fu guru Chop Chop Master Onion, party flea MC King Kong Mushi, and moose drill sergeant Instructor Moosesha. Each brings their own flavor to the mix, and Parappa must keep up if he wants to complete their stage in style.

To become a hip hop superstar, players help Parappa match the rhythm of the current song and rap his lyrics at the proper time. When a master spits their dope rhyme, icons for buttons appear on screen and players must repeat back the sequence while staying on the beat. Too many off-beat lyrics and it's game over for you and poor Parappa. Like many old-school rhythm titles, the Parappa the Rapper series can be very unforgiving. You may have to try each song a few times before you truly get the rhythm down. The games don't have lots of tracks, but catchy lyrics and multiple difficulty levels will keep true rhythm veterans coming back for more. If your rap game is off the chain, then step up to the challenge!

WHAT TO PLAY NEXT:
Gitaroo Man
Elite Beat Agents
The DJ Hero series

TOP SERIES PICKS:
Parappa the Rapper (PS, 1996)
Parappa the Rapper 2 (PS2, 2001)
Parappa the Rapper HD (PS4, 2017)

YOU'LL LIKE THESE GAMES IF...
You spit hot fire on the mic.

Played it! ☐   My Rating: ☆☆☆☆☆

My Favorite Moment: _____

Notes: _____

_____

98

ELITE BEAT AGENTS

PLAY IT ON:
DS

GENRE:
Party & Rhythm

RATING:
E10+

FIRST SEEN:
2006

MADE BY:
Nintendo

Everyone can use a little cheering up when things aren't going their way. What could be more cheerful than a group of dancing and singing cheerleaders? And not your everyday pom-pom waving cheerleaders, but special cheer agents with a mission to bring joy and confidence into everyday settings.

The Elite Beat Agents series began in Japan as *Osu! Tatakae! Ouendan* (which translates to *Go! Fight! Cheer Squad*) for the Nintendo DS. The game features an all-male trio of cheerleaders who wear traditional Japanese school uniforms and use their catchy performances to help average people with their daily problems. It was such a hit that it was remade for DS owners across the globe.

Elite Beat Agents introduced a new cheer squad, including agents J, Spin, Morris, Derek, and Chieftain. This dedicated team of well-dressed hype men must cheer on struggling babysitters, movie stars, magicians, and more. To help them with their mission, players must tap, trace, and spin different markers to the beat of an inspirational song. Each musical track is tied to a story, which advances in a comic book fashion on the top screen. Put a little pep in your step and you might just brighten someone's day!

DID YOU KNOW?

In 2008, the 20th anniversary issue of *Nintendo Power* listed the top 20 games for each of Nintendo's past systems. *Elite Beat Agents* was ranked as the number one Nintendo DS game of all time, beating out classic series like Pokémon, Zelda, and Mario.

Played it! ☐   My Rating: ☆☆☆☆☆
My Favorite Moment: _____
Notes: _____
_____

BIT.TRIP

The blips and bloops of old school games inspired the Bit.Trip series. The original six games, which can all be found in the collection *The Bit.Trip*, focus on simple pixel graphics and catchy chiptune music. Each title has its own unique style of rhythm gameplay and a library of funky beats.

The most popular entries in the Bit.Trip series are the games that focus on Commander Video, the speedy mascot. This lanky black and white alien is the star of the Bit.Trip Runner titles, most famously *Runner2: Future Legend of Rhythm Alien*. The Bit.Trip Runner games are designed around Commander Video's ability to sprint, slide, kick, and jump past obstacles to the beat of a futuristic groove. If the commander comes in contact with any of the many hurdles in his way, he's flung all the way back to his last checkpoint. While the Bit.Trip Runner titles began with retro-inspired pixel visuals, they have evolved into a vibrant 3D rhythm relay. With the launch of *Runner3* in 2017, developers Choice Provisions gave rhythm fans even more to cheer about with loads of new characters, levels, and unlockables. If you can stay on the beat, you can stay on your feet.

PLAY IT ON:
Switch, PS4, iOS, and more

GENRE:
Party & Rhythm

RATING:
E-T

FIRST SEEN:
2009

DID YOU KNOW?

In 2013, a downloadable character pack called *Good Friends* was released for *Runner2*. It features playable oddballs from fan favorite series such as Cave Story, Psychonauts, and Portal.

MADE BY:
Choice Provisions

Played it! ☐ My Rating: ☆☆☆☆☆

My Favorite Moment: _____

Notes: _____

_____

100

HATSUNE MIKU

PLAY IT ON:
PS4, 3DS, PSVita,
and more

GENRE:
Party &
Rhythm

RATING:
E10+-T

**FIRST
SEEN:**
2009

MADE BY:
SEGA

There are plenty of talented musicians that sadly can't hold a tune when it comes to singing. This is exactly why the Yamaha Corporation developed a program called *Vocaloid*, computer software that can perfectly imitate a singing voice. The Vocaloid technology can even match different types of pitch, vibrato, and tone depending on the type of song. Hatsune Miku is the

DID YOU KNOW?
In 2010, over 14,000 people petitioned to send the virtual pop-star into space, so an aluminum plate etched with pictures of Hatsune Miku was launched into space aboard a Japanese Venus spacecraft explorer.

famous pop-star mascot of the Vocaloid programs, and in 2009 she took the stage in her first rhythm video game titled *Project DIVA*.

Since the original launch, nearly a dozen Hatsune Miku titles have been released. Each game features new songs created using the Vocaloid program and showcases Hatsune Miku's range of musical genres—the newest Hatsune Miku title, *Project DIVA Future Tone* for PlayStation 4, has over 220 songs for rhythm masters to complete! The series has had huge success in Japan and has spread to many different corners of the world, with more and more music fans falling in love with the long-haired virtual idol.

When it comes to gameplay, the Hatsune Miku series is similar to other rhythm titles—players must attempt to line up incoming notes to the beat of a pumped up song. The main difference is that the notes aren't on a track of any kind (with the exception of a few games in the series), and instead come flying from all different sides of the screen. Players have to keep their focus and react quickly if they want to hit every note and keep their score multiplier going.

With a name that translates to "the first sound from the future," Hatsune Miku is certainly making the future of music look bright.

WHAT TO PLAY NEXT:
The Dance Dance Revolution series
Theatrhythm Final Fantasy: Curtain Call
VOEZ

TOP SERIES PICKS:
Hatsune Miku: Project Mirai DX (3DS, 2015)
Hatsune Miku: Project DIVA X (PS4, 2016)
Hatsune Miku: Future Tone (PS4, 2017)

YOU'LL LIKE THESE GAMES IF...
You have superstar stage presence.

Played it! ☐   My Rating: ☆☆☆☆☆

My Favorite Moment: _____

Notes: _____

_____

101

JUST DANCE

PLAY IT ON:
Switch, PS4,
XOne, and more

GENRE:
Party & Rhythm

RATING:
E–E10+

**FIRST
SEEN:**
2009

MADE BY:
Ubisoft

Before the introduction of special dance pads and motion controls, it was impossible for gamers to score points while they shook their booty. Luckily, we now live in an age where rhythm games can perfectly follow your funky dance moves.

The Just Dance series began as an exclusive title for the Nintendo Wii in 2010. The original game uses the Wiimote's motion controls to track various moves and poses that are unique to the selected song. While a crew of colorful silhouettes perform the current dance to perfection, upcoming motions are shown in the corner of the screen. With a new song, you never know what kind of groove you'll be in for, so be ready for anything.

Since its debut, the Just Dance series has sold millions of copies and spread to every home console imaginable. New Just Dance titles even let players use their cell phone as a way to track their motions. Hits by top artists like Beyoncé, Katy Perry, Jason Derulo, and even Hatsune Miku (turn back a page) have been featured in the Just Dance lineup. It's always more fun to dance with friends, so grab a buddy and get ready to boogie!

DID YOU KNOW?

The idea for Just Dance came from a minigame called *Dancing with Dweebs* in the Rayman Raving Rabbids series, where players mimic the dance moves of a silver stick figure while wacky rabbit judges nod to the beat.

Played it! ☐ My Rating: ☆☆☆☆☆

My Favorite Moment: _____

Notes: _____

_____